A Beautiful Way

An Invitation to a Jesus-Centered Life

Dan Baumann
with Mark Klassen

YWAM
PUBLISHING
P.O. Box 55787 / Seattle, WA 98155

YWAM Publishing is the publishing ministry of Youth With A Mission. Youth With A Mission (YWAM) is an international missionary organization of Christians from many denominations dedicated to presenting Jesus Christ to this generation. To this end, YWAM has focused its efforts in three main areas: (1) training and equipping believers for their part in fulfilling the Great Commission (Matthew 28:19), (2) personal evangelism, and (3) mercy ministry (medical and relief work).

For a free catalog of books and materials, contact:

YWAM Publishing
P.O. Box 55787, Seattle, WA 98155
(425) 771-1153 or (800) 922-2143
www.ywampublishing.com

Library of Congress Cataloging-in-Publication Data

Baumann, Dan, 1963–
  A beautiful way : an invitation to a Jesus-centered life / by Dan Baumann with Mark Klassen.— 1st ed.
    p. cm.
  ISBN 1-57658-312-0
  1. Spiritual life—Christianity. 2. Christian life. 3. God. I. Klassen, Mark, 1967– II. Title.
  BV4501.3.B39 2004
  248.4—dc22   2004021550

A Beautiful Way: An Invitation to a Jesus-Centered Life
Copyright © 2005 by Dan Baumann

10 09 08 07 06 05   10 9 8 7 6 5 4 3 2 1

Published by Youth With A Mission Publishing
P.O. Box 55787, Seattle, WA 98155

ISBN 1-57658-312-0

Please see page 175 for the copyright notices of all Bible versions used in this book and for an explanation of the abbreviations of their names.

Printed in China

❦ dedications

To my dear friends, Randy and Edie Thomas. Thank you so much for all your love and for your encouragement over the years to teach and encourage young people to find "A Beautiful Way." I am so grateful that you have believed in me and released me to do what God has asked me to do.

—Dan

To Alexis Ayn and Dania Kay, my beautiful daughters, in hopes that you will learn to love Jesus and that you will lead others in your generation to discover the beauty of following him.

—Mark

✎ acknowledgements

From Dan

I want to thank my friends at YWAM Trinidad, Colorado, who helped me with this project. Pete, Josanna, Becky, Edie, Jessica, Tasha, Cat, thanks for all your help and input. I also want to thank Misha and Lionel Thompson and Geoff and Janet Benge for your input into the book.

I want to thank my parents, Hans and Gunila Baumann. I love you! Thanks so much for believing in me and encouraging me to see this project happen.

I want to deeply thank Mark Klassen for helping me write this book. Your friendship, godliness, and commitment to excellence have inspired me greatly. Thank so much for all the long hours you have invested into this book. Thanks too for modeling the message of *A Beautiful Way.*

I want to thank Amy Klassen and Alexis and Dania Klassen for releasing Mark to work many hours on this project.

I want to thank Tom, Warren, Marit, and all of the staff of YWAM Publishing. Thanks for believing in Mark and me and encouraging us to write this book.

I want to thank Loren Cunningham, the founder of YWAM. Two years ago, you challenged me to write a second book. Your words have been a deep source of encouragement to me.

Mostly, I want to thank my Lord and Savior Jesus Christ. You are "A Beautiful Way." It's all about you!

From Mark

It's one thing to be blessed with good friends; it's another thing to be blessed with the opportunity to work closely with those friends. I thank God for the opportunity I've had to work with Dan Baumann on this book. Thanks, Dan, for giving me a chance and letting me help. You are an inspiration to me in many ways, but nothing impresses me more than your simple love for Jesus.

Our friends at YWAM Publishing, especially Warren and Marit, have been so positive and helpful throughout the process. Thanks also to Janet Benge for reviewing an early draft for us and gently suggesting needed improvements.

I'd like to express appreciation to my friend and present employer, Frank Ens, who gave me much freedom and encouragement during the writing. I'd also like to thank my friend Jonathan Quapp, who has faithfully stood by me in prayer throughout these past couple of years, including the year of writing. Thanks also to my family, both sets of parents and siblings, who have consistently shown interest in this book and offered valuable support and encouragement along the way. And to Dave Manuel, Ryan Harder, Greg Watt, Darrel Spenst, and Larry Wiebe, thanks for your friendship over the years and for encouraging me, each in your own way, to write.

Spouses often receive the final acknowledgement in book writing, and now I know why. No one in my life has sacrificed more during this project than my wife, Amy. At times it has been challenging for us, but she has amazed me once again with her patience and grace. Amy, I love you.

🔥 contents

🔥 introduction

Dear friends,

Jesus said, "I am the way" (John 14:6), and those who follow him discover that it is a *beautiful* way.

As Christians we are all on this journey of discovery. We are being convinced that we have found in Jesus something that is far more beautiful than anything we have ever experienced or imagined. As I sit down to write, I am excited about the opportunity I have to share my heart with you as it relates to the incredible journey we are on.

In 2001 my first book, *Imprisoned in Iran*, was published. It tells the story of my trip into Iran to explore possible service opportunities, my nine weeks in prison on a false charge, and my miraculous release. Since then I have had the privilege of sharing my story in many different settings around the world. As I have done this, many people have asked me, "How did you ever get from living in California to being in prison in the Middle East? Tell us about your walk with God and how Jesus has led you." Those questions have challenged me to think more about the experiences and principles that have shaped my own walk with God and also about how I could more effectively share my faith journey with others. This second book, then, is the result of that thinking.

This book has three parts: Believing, Trusting, and Serving. They represent key aspects of the spiritual life: learning to believe the truth about God's character, interacting with God in ways that nurture trust, and then giving ourselves in service to others. Although there often seems to be a logical progression from one to the other, these areas are interrelated in terms of how God transforms our lives, and God's dealings with us cannot necessarily be traced specifically in this order. It is my hope that as you read each part, God will use it to continue the work of transformation that he is doing in your life.

Most of all, *A Beautiful Way* is an invitation to a relationship. It's about following Jesus. It is not an invitation to a career in global missions. Though this is the calling God has chosen for me and for many others, the principles that I write about apply equally to those who are working a nine-to-five job, those who are going to school, or those who are working at home. Whatever your career or life situation, you are invited to embrace a life that is completely centered on the person of Jesus.

My heart longs for each one of us to discover more and more of the life that Jesus offers to us and to let go of everything that distracts us and prevents us from finding it. It is with this longing that I want to share my own journey with you and invite you to walk alongside me as we explore *a beautiful way* together.

Your brother,
Dan

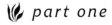 *part one*

Believing

The journey begins with believing. *More than simply belief in God's existence, I want to address belief in terms of how we understand God's character and how this affects our relationship with him. No one can expect to find* a beautiful way *unless they encounter the God who freely offers it to them and longs for them to find it. Chapters 1 and 2 focus on two key aspects of God's character: his personal love and his goodness. There is, of course, more to God than these two characteristics, but these are crucial for us to understand, and it seems to me that many Christians today are in the midst of a great struggle within themselves to believe these things about God.*

For great is your love toward me.

—Psalm 86:13

This is love: not that we loved God,
but that he loved us and sent his Son
as an atoning sacrifice for our sins.

—1 John 4:10

chapter one

God's Personal Love

*G*od always takes the first step. Before we ever loved God, he loved us. Before we ever invited him into our lives, he extended an invitation to us. Without that invitation we would be without hope. If God were not interested in being in relationship with us, we would have absolutely no way of reaching him and no chance at all of discovering meaning for our lives. We would be lost.

As Christians we believe in God as the Great Initiator. There is nothing more foundational to our faith than the belief that God is reaching out to us in love. Nothing else brings more meaning to human existence than the fact that our Creator is committed to initiating relationship with us.

It is this *downward* motion—God toward us—
that distinguishes Christianity from all other reli-
gions. Instead of us reaching up to heaven to find
God, we believe that God is reaching down to earth
to find us. Our Creator has not left us alone to figure
out why we are here. There is meaning to our lives:
we are loved by God.

> *"Everything you do for God will be
> the overflow of intimacy with God."*

A Christian high-school student was once told,
"Everything you do for God will be the overflow of
intimacy with God." The statement made an impact
on the young man. After hearing it, he pondered long
and hard over what intimacy with God could mean.
Deep in thought, he walked down to a nearby river
and began to throw rocks. As another rock splashed
into the river, the young man heard an inner voice
ask the question, *Can I throw rocks with you?*

He didn't think much of it at first, but when he
heard it again, he questioned himself about whether
or not it could be the voice of God. He quickly concluded that it could not be, convincing himself easily

that God was not interested in such a mundane activity. But he kept hearing the voice over and over again, until finally he stopped, turned to heaven, and said, "God, I think you're asking to throw rocks with me. But why? Why would you want to throw rocks with me? I mean, you're concerned about the world and all its problems. You can't possibly care about throwing rocks with me."

Then he heard the voice again, with even greater clarity, *I want to throw rocks with you because you want to throw rocks. I just want to hang out with you and do whatever you are doing. I just want us to be together so that our friendship can grow.*

In amazement, the young man replied, "That's it?" believing now that he was actually talking to Jesus.

That's it, Jesus replied.

It was on that day that I—Dan Baumann, a normal fifteen-year-old—began to realize that Jesus was madly in love with me. He loved me when I was having my personal devotions or sharing my faith, but he was just as much in love with me when I was relaxing, watching a movie, or throwing rocks. Jesus loved me without conditions and without restraints! From that day forward, as an ordinary kid growing up in Southern California, I became more and more aware of Jesus' personal love for me. More than anything else, Jesus wanted to be my friend and to hang out with me at every possible opportunity. I was totally amazed! How could the God of the universe love me like that!? Wow! What do you do when you are loved like that? For me, in that moment, I was changed, and all I wanted to do was to love God back.

God's great love sets us free to respond.

Maybe you have had your own experience like this, when God revealed to you how much he loves you. It may have been similar to mine, or it may have been very different. It may have also been a series of experiences. Maybe these experiences are etched forever in your heart, or maybe you have allowed their details to become clouded with negative experiences. We need to recall these moments in our lives when God's personal love became real for us. And if we don't feel we've ever experienced this kind of affirmation from God, we need to ask God for our own evidence of his personal love. He is more than eager to answer this kind of request.

The love of God is at work all around us. Of course, from our human perspective, we don't always see all of what God is doing on our behalf. When he is actively drawing us to himself, we can be quite unaware of it. When he was choosing us, we didn't know about it. When he was softening our hearts toward him, we didn't understand what was happening within us. This is why, in many cases, we talk about how we found God rather than how God found us. But when we come to faith and accept the perspective of the Scriptures, we learn to believe that God's action comes prior to our action. We still grapple with the mystery of it all, but we agree with the words of Jesus, "No one can come to me unless the Father who sent me draws him" (John 6:44). When we are personally awakened by God's loving action toward us, we realize that our role in the relationship is one of *response*. God's great love sets us free to respond. It invites a reply. God speaks; we answer. He acts; we react.

This understanding of God as the Initiator helps us to maintain a God-centered perspective on our lives of faith. It saves us from thinking that it's all up to us. We must be careful not to be led astray to believe that our salvation is the result of anything other than God's initiation. When the apostle Paul writes about our salvation, he says, "It's God's gift from start to finish! We don't play the major role" (Eph. 2:8–9, MSG). The apostle John also goes to great lengths to protect us from a self-centered spirituality when he emphasizes in the fourth chapter of his first letter that "love comes from God" (vs. 7), that "God is love" (vss. 8, 16), and that "we love because he first loved us" (vs. 19). The only way to understand our Christian lives is to begin with God's love toward us, not our love toward him.

Nothing exhibits God's love and his commitment to relationship more than the sending of his Son, Jesus Christ: "This is how God showed his love among us: He sent his one and only Son into the world that we might live through him" (1 John 4:9). God could not have made it more clear to us. In the sacrificial death of Jesus, God spoke to us, saying, "I love you, and I have made a way for us to be in relationship with each other."

The death was necessary because of sin. According to God's law, "without the shedding of blood there is no forgiveness" (Heb. 9:22). But instead of the temporary substitution of animal sacrifices, which were offered regularly according to the Old Testament law, Jesus Christ came to earth to die as the perfect sacrifice, offered once for all. Instead of us facing our own death sentence because of our sin, Christ faced it for us. And in providing a way for us to be forgiven, God dealt with the one thing that kept us distant from him. He made it possible for us to be together with him, to be at peace with him. That's what atonement is all about. Our sin separated us from him. We were estranged, alienated from our Creator. In fact, we were dead in our sin, unable to help ourselves, unable on our own to remedy our hopeless situation. We needed God to make a move toward us. In Jesus, he did. The apostle Paul says that "God was reconciling the world to himself in Christ" (2 Cor. 5:19).

This commitment to relationship becomes even more amazing to us once we understand that, in our sinful state, we were not only helpless before God but hostile toward him. In our sin we were enemies of God (Rom. 5:10). Thankfully, God loves his enemies. As we pushed him away, he was still reaching out to us. Through the death of Christ, he effected a transformation on our behalf, changing us from his enemies into his friends. He disarmed us, not through coercion but through an amazing act of unconditional love. Paul says that "God demonstrates his own love for us in this: While we were still sinners, Christ died for us" (Rom. 5:8). God did not wait for us to clean up our lives before he saved us. Contrary to the common *un*biblical saying, God helps those who *cannot* help themselves.

Where does this leave us? What does it do for you, to know that God loves you like this? How will you respond to God's loving invitation to relationship? Even though God has made the first move, there comes a time when he waits for us to move.

Sometimes, however, we hesitate. We doubt. We resist God's love. Even though we may easily and eagerly admit to the facts about God's love for humanity, somehow we still find it hard to believe that God is deeply in love with each one of us as individuals. As we look within ourselves, we sometimes struggle with the idea that God's love is personal and he wants to prove this love to each one of us in specific ways. Instead of living under the power and freedom of God's affirmation, we allow ourselves to focus on our own inadequacies and limitations. One of the ways it becomes evident is when, at the end of the day, our minds dwell on two things: what we have done and what we haven't done. Hopelessly we evaluate the day based on the tasks that we did or did not accomplish, and more often than not, we feel guilty about both or either of these things. This leaves us going to bed at night feeling insecure, anxious, and unloved.

If you are like me, you have often struggled with this kind of heaviness. It was during my years at university that these pressures began to take their toll on me. After I graduated from high school in Southern California, I attended a Christian school in Illinois called Wheaton College. It was there that I began to learn how important it was for me to get beyond my own cramped perspective and take into account *God's* perspective on my life.

Basically, I learned to go to bed at night with one thought on my mind, and that was "God loves me." There is nothing else more important than that. Learning to rest in God's love changed me. It brought me peace and security that nothing else could bring.

Although God is not ignorant of your failures, he does not focus on them.

No matter what has happened in your day, Jesus wants you to go to bed at night remembering that one simple truth, "God loves you." Although God is not ignorant of your failures, he does not focus on them. Because of what Jesus accomplished on the cross, you are justified in God's eyes. He is consumed with a love for you and wants you to be assured of that love at the end of every day.

I can already hear many of you saying, "But..." Yes, we can all think of many reasons why God shouldn't love us, but the simple truth is, he does. No matter what has happened today, he loves you. He loves you as you close your eyes to sleep, and he is excited in the morning as you begin another day with him.

God invites us to experience a love without limits, a love that is not based on what we do.

We need to make it a practice to remind ourselves of God's love for us each night before we go to bed. Maybe we need to read a psalm, sing a worship song, or even just say, simply, "Thank you, God, for loving me."

When we do this, it helps us to rest in God's love. It also prepares us for our tomorrow. Knowing that God's mercies are new every morning (Lam. 3:23), we can move on from our yesterday, even when it is tainted by failure. So often, we cause ourselves to come under a heaviness that leads to depression and disillusionment because we are so inwardly focused and lose sight of his unconditional love for us. God invites us to experience a love without limits, a love that is not based on what we do.

Despite this open invitation from God, it is often difficult to maintain this understanding. If you are like me, it is a constant struggle.

After I graduated from college in 1988, I joined an international missions organization called Youth With A Mission (YWAM). Over the years I traveled extensively with the mission and actively pursued a variety of service opportunities.

Once while I was with YWAM in the States, I had an experience that tested my grasp of God's love for me. I was relaxing and playing billiards one day when a thought ran through my head: *Am I really doing what's best right now? I could be serving God overseas or preaching somewhere. What am I doing here playing this game? Am I missing God's best?*

As I thought about it, I was reminded of the simple truth that God's love for us is not based on what we *do*. God does not love us more because we are doing something we may consider more spiritual or useful. My feelings of guilt were based not on the truth of God's unconditional love but rather on the idea that I could somehow earn that love. As I continued to play billiards, I worked through some of this in my mind and began to affirm some simple truths: *Nothing can separate me from the love of God. He loves me right now! Nothing I do can make God love me more. Nothing I do can make God love me less.* As I pondered these things, the peace of God filled my heart and mind.

The more we understand God's love, the more we will want to love him back.

Of course God's love for us should not inspire laziness. We will look at this later in the book, but the issue here is our motivation—why we do the things we do. What happened to me while I was playing billiards was that I had a greater revelation of his love for me. The more we understand God's love, the more we will want to love him back. Our actions, then, are to be inspired by love and gratitude and not by some sense of guilt or obligation.

Two stories early in the Gospel of John beautifully demonstrate the personal love that Jesus has for each one of us. The fourth chapter (vss. 1–42) describes Jesus' encounter with a woman at a well. As the woman of Samaria approaches the well, Jesus initiates the conversation with a simple question: "Will you give me a drink?" We are told in the text (vs. 9) that Jews did not associate with Samaritans, and the woman's response to Jesus reveals her genuine surprise: "You are a Jew and I am a Samaritan woman. How can you ask me for a drink?"

Jesus then turns the conversation away from the water in the well to a "living water" that he is eager to share with the woman. The woman is intrigued by the offer and is drawn deeper into conversation with this man Jesus. When he begins to mysteriously expose some relationship problems in her personal life and history, the woman perceives that she is indeed speaking with someone very special. But still there are significant things that separate them, most importantly their religion. When Jesus judiciously breaks down this barrier as well and convinces her that his offer of life is equally open to Samaritans, she can do nothing but receive his love.

Despite a variety of reasons why Jesus shouldn't interact with this woman, he communicates a deep and personal love for her, a love that transforms her. Jesus boldly breaks down barriers of race, religion, sex, and reputation and calls this woman to a life of meaning and wholeness. Even though Jesus knows her personal flaws and frailty, he accepts her and wins her heart. And it is this love that inspires her and finally commissions her to invite others to meet this man and to experience his love.

Even though there are many things that legitimately separate you from Jesus, not least of which are your personal failings, Jesus loves you and is eager to convince you of his personal love.

The next chapter of John (5:1–15, MSG) tells a similar story of transformation. This time Jesus approaches a man at the Pool of Bethesda. The man has been ill and sitting beside the pool for thirty-eight years when Jesus asks him, "Do you want to get well?"

The man answers, "Sir, when the water is stirred, I don't have anybody to put me in the pool. By the time I get there, somebody else is already in." This man only sees one way to get well, and he can't achieve it. He has tried many times but it eludes his grasp. You can hear the hopelessness in his voice.

Then Jesus tells the man, "Get up, take your bedroll, start walking" (vs. 8). And the man is healed. He is instantly able to pick up his mat and walk.

Jesus comes to this man to bless him, to meet his need. When all hope is gone and there seems to be no other way, Jesus appears on the scene. He walks into our lives in the same way. He comes to heal and to make whole. This is who Jesus is. He is very committed to our personal lives, whatever needs and desires we have. He knows what we long for, and he longs to grant us our requests even before we ask. The man beside the pool thought he was forgotten, but he wasn't. Even though you may at times feel the same way, forgotten and without hope, Jesus is there for you.

What would you say if God said to you, "What do you want?"

For the lame man by the pool, I'm sure Jesus' question, "Do you want to get well?" came as a surprise. *Who was this man, asking such bold questions?* We need to understand that God desires to interact with each one of us in this kind of intensely personal way. What would you say if God said to you, "What do you want?" Are you ready and willing to be specific with God?

A young woman named Debbie had recently been challenged by another believer to ask God to reveal himself to her in a very specific way. Debbie responded to the challenge and prayed silently to God, asking him to give her a dozen long-stem, peach-colored roses and a ring for her finger that would be a reminder of his personal love for her.

After a few days a van pulled up to the place where Debbie worked. The driver told the secretary at the front desk that he was working for a florist and there had been a mistake in their order that day. They had some extra long-stem, peach-colored roses, and he wondered if anyone there could possibly make use of them.

Not knowing anything about Debbie's prayer, the secretary decided to surprise her friend and fellow believer with the roses. She accepted the roses from the driver; then, with a borrowed key, she slipped into Debbie's apartment and put an arrangement of a dozen long-stem, peach-colored roses into a vase.

When Debbie walked into her apartment later that day, she was overwhelmed by the specific answer to her prayer.

Shortly afterward a Christian couple who had been friends with Debbie for some time invited her out for dinner. At dinner they shared with her that recently they had had an impression that they should give her something, a special gift that had been in their family for many years. They handed her a box, and inside was a beautiful diamond ring. Overwhelmed again, Debbie put on the ring. She wore it as a reminder of God's personal love for her.

God wants to prove himself to each one of us. It may not be the same for you as it was for Debbie, but he wants to show you that he loves you.

One recent example from my own life came in the fall of 2002. I was asking God for a new Bible, and I felt like he was challenging me to be specific about what I wanted. So I asked specifically for a navy blue NIV Study Bible. I even specified that it didn't need to be brand new. After praying, I was content to see how God would provide. A week later, however, I was near a Christian bookstore and thought that maybe I should just buy my new Bible. As I walked through the doors, I felt God encourage me to wait for his provision in another way. The following week I had a similar experience at another bookstore in another city. Again I felt God say, *Wait.* But this time I also felt that he said the Bible would be provided for me next week during my visit to Texas. Sure enough, on the last day of my visit to a church in Waco, my hosts, unaware of my prayer request, took me to a lost and found box in the church and asked simply if I needed a Bible. When I said that I did, they answered, "Take whichever one you want."

I looked down into the box, and right before my eyes was a used navy blue NIV Study Bible. Go, God!

———————

*Ask God to surprise you today
with how much he loves you.*

———————

Does God want to surprise you with his personal love in very specific ways? I want to challenge you to ask God to surprise you today with how much he loves you.

On another occasion God allowed me to be involved with one of his personal surprises for someone else, a man named Mark.

I met Mark in 1998 in New York, one year after I had returned to the United States after a harrowing experience in prison in Iran. In 1997 I had traveled into Iran with a friend of mine named Glenn to explore the possibility of future service opportunities within the country. On my way out of the country, I was detained by Iranian authorities and put into prison unjustly, charged with espionage. I was imprisoned for nine weeks before I was miraculously released.

I will tell more of my experiences in prison in the pages that follow, but upon my return to the States,

I had many opportunities to share my story. On one occasion I was asked to speak in a church in New York. As I prayed about the invitation, I felt quite sure that I should go. However, as I walked into that church on a Sunday evening, dressed in my typical casual attire, I immediately felt out of place. The feeling was probably so strong because everything else in the church building seemed to me to be perfectly in place, including every man and boy in a suit and tie. When the pastor approached me, he looked me up and down and, with disdain in his voice, asked, "Are you the guest speaker?"

"Yes," I said hesitantly.

"Just give us your testimony about getting out of prison," he replied abruptly, leaving little doubt that he was expecting someone more impressive than me.

Struggling with uneasiness and insecurity, all I wanted was for that service to end and to quickly get on a plane heading home. But after I finished sharing my story, I was approached by a man who greeted me with tears in his eyes. He began, "Sir, my name is Mark, and I'm not from here. I was driving through this town tonight when I felt the Lord challenge me to walk into this church and listen to the preacher. A few weeks ago, God spoke to me about making restitution for several crimes that I had committed before I was saved. I did what God told me to do, but tomorrow I go into prison to serve a three-year sentence. After hearing you speak tonight, I know that the Lord will help me and that he will give me strength to endure."

Mark and I embraced, and we prayed together. As I left the church that evening, I had no doubt about why God had brought me there. I was greatly encouraged as I thought about God's personal love for Mark. What a privilege to be a part of God's surprise in his life.

Even though God holds the entire universe together, he also watches over each and every individual.

The personal love that God has for each one of us is shown in many and various ways. Sometimes God brings us special encouragement. Sometimes he provides exactly what we need. Sometimes God shows his love for us in how he protects us from harm. Even though God holds the entire universe together, he also watches over each and every individual. Many times I have been amazed to see God's hand of protection upon my life.

Between 1988 and 1993, while serving with YWAM, I helped administer an eye hospital in Kabul, Afghanistan. On one occasion I went with a team from the hospital to run an eye clinic in the north-eastern part of the country. The village where we were based was high up in the mountains (11,000 feet above sea level), and we had to walk for two days just to get there. The mountain trail was narrow and dangerous. On the way I tripped on a rock and stumbled off the trail. I fell onto a smooth boulder and quickly began to slide down the side of it. There was nothing to stop me, and as I glanced down, all I could see was a drop of at least one hundred feet below me. In a panic I cried out to God. As I continued to slide, I could see a little six-inch shrub sticking out of the rock. In desperation I grabbed for it, and to my amazement it held me and stopped me from falling. I held on to it long enough to gather my senses and to find a crack in the rock where I could brace myself. From there I slowly climbed back onto the trail. Once on the trail again, I looked down at the tiny shrub, knowing that it was nothing short of a miracle that it had kept me from plunging over the cliff. Somehow God had intervened and saved my life!

However, that is only part of the story of God's intervention at that moment in my life. Three years later, Maria, a friend from Brazil, approached me and inquired bluntly about my safety three years earlier, "Dan, were you ever in danger of losing your life back then?"

I immediately recalled the accident on the trail in the mountains of Afghanistan. "Yes," I said, "I almost fell off a cliff."

Maria then proceeded to tell me about the night three years earlier when she was awakened from her sleep and prompted by God to pray for my safety and for the sparing of my life. This kind of thing happened very rarely in her life, so she was careful to journal the details of the awakening. As we talked further and compared notes, we concurred that Maria had been called to pray at the precise time I was in danger on the trail!

God cares deeply for each one of us. He loves us in a profoundly personal way. I believe that he is prepared to convince us of that in ways that are quite obvious. We only need to open the door to the possibilities.

In Revelation the apostle John records an invitation from Jesus: "Behold, I stand at the door and knock; if anyone hears my voice and opens the door, I will come in to him and eat with him, and he with me" (Rev. 3:20, RSV). Jesus desires this kind of intimacy with each and every believer. He invites each one of us to open the door and to experience his personal love for us. As we do, we will be changed forever.

🌿 How great is your goodness, which you have stored up for those who fear you.

—*Psalm 31:19*

🌿 Taste and see that the LORD is good. Oh, the joys of those who trust in him!

—*Psalm 34:8* (NLT)

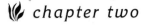 *chapter two*

God's Goodness

God is for you. He has your best interests in mind. He wants you to find enjoyment in life. God is good, and he wants each of us to experience his goodness. This is exactly what the Bible affirms again and again, both in the New and the Old Testaments. Throughout biblical history God's people celebrate God's goodness.

Despite these affirmations, we sometimes still think of God as a tyrant, someone who is withholding good from us and trying to make things difficult for us. We may not say it, but sometimes we think it. Is it possible that God is mean rather than good? Does he have cruel intentions? Do you sometimes think that he is trying to make life miserable for you?

During my imprisonment in Iran, I questioned God's goodness. I was innocent of the crimes of which I was accused, but would God come to my defense? In the midst of my loneliness and despair, it was an incredible struggle for me to acknowledge that it was God's good intention to bless me there in prison. I had believed in the goodness of God, but now I was confronted with something that threatened to disprove it. Alone in my prison cell, I was miserable. I thought I might never again see my friends and family. I thought I might never again walk freely in the sunshine. I was beaten regularly, and I could often hear others being beaten and even executed. I was stricken by fear, knowing that, at any moment, I might be the next to be executed. Often I lay curled up in the corner of my cell, shaking, crying, and cringing at any sound. Even though God had rescued me from many other difficult situations in the past, there in prison my hope was gone. I believed that this time God would *not* deliver me. And there was nothing within me that could muster up the faith to believe otherwise. Despair had set in at its deepest level.

For those who have read my prison story, you know about the day when this despair drove me to attempt suicide in my cell. It was only by God's grace that my attempt failed. Afterward, as I lay on the ground sobbing, Jesus met me in a miraculous way. I knew in that moment that Jesus was with me and that he would carry me through the rest of my time in prison.

Through that experience I began to realize that no matter how much pain and loss I was suffering, I still had what was most important to me—my relationship with God. Even though I had lost most of the other things that brought meaning and enjoyment to my life, no one could take away my faith. No one could separate me from God.

As I turned to the Scriptures there in my cell, particularly the psalms and the gospels, my faith was renewed. I saw in the lives of David and Jesus the understanding that even while we are experiencing pain and loss in other areas of our lives, we can still experience joy in our relationship with God. In fact, it is the pain that pushes us to God. It depends entirely on what we see as most important. There in prison God was challenging my values and clarifying for me what was ultimately most essential for my well-being.

Though it was a painful process, I was truly thankful for what I was learning. I was growing closer to God, and as my vision of Jesus became more and more clear, my circumstances became less and less significant. Though my situation didn't change, my perspective did. In the gloom of my cell, once again I was able to say with confidence that God is good.

God is committed to doing something good in each of us. He is committed to cultivating growth in our lives.

Think about the trials you have encountered in life. What have you learned from them? How have you been strengthened through them? If you value the development of Christian character in your life, then you will be able to endure trials with this godly purpose in mind. It doesn't necessarily decrease the pain you may experience in the midst of the trial, but it will give you perspective. It will allow you to see beyond the immediate pain and to find joy and solace in God.

This is what James writes about in his letter to the churches: "Consider it pure joy, my brothers, whenever you face trials of many kinds" (James 1:2). Why? That sounds almost crazy unless we, like James, place a high value on spiritual growth and maturity.

According to James, the reason why you should get excited about difficulty in your life is simply, "because you know that the testing of your faith develops perseverance....so that you may be mature and complete" (vss. 3–4).

Whatever the source of difficulty in our lives, God is committed to doing something good in each of us. He is committed to cultivating growth in our lives. If we understand this, we will be able to endure the times of testing, but if we lose sight of God's good intent, the difficulties in life will drag us down and we will resist God's purpose.

A friend of mine, Misha, was only twenty-one years old when doctors told her she might never walk again. They also told her it would be impossible for her to have children. She had already suffered for years with a debilitating condition, and now she was losing hope. Twenty-three different medications and supplements had been prescribed to help her deal with the pain, but she was exhausted both physically and emotionally. She was afraid of becoming bitter and didn't want to allow anger to delude her. Maybe worst of all, she felt very alone. Misha's faith pushed her toward God, but she wasn't sure what to expect from him. Bedridden, she was isolated from her friends. She hoped to be married, but who would ever want to marry her like this? At times she was afraid of what she would do to herself if she got really hopeless, and for that reason she would not keep her medications next to her bed.

It was in the midst of this despair that God spoke to Misha, asking her, *Do you believe that I am good?* At first she didn't know how to take the question. Misha knew God existed. She had experienced his love. She was committed to following him. But the question about his goodness was difficult for her. She thought about war, about cancer, about poverty. She thought about her own challenging situation and the pain she was experiencing. It was easy to question the goodness of God, but she also knew that there was plenty of evidence that he is good. For Misha it came down to a simple choice. She chose to believe in God's goodness. She chose to embrace what he had allowed in her life. She reasoned within herself that if it was by faith that she believed in God's existence, and by accepting what the Bible said, and by testing it with her own experience, then she would have to wrestle in the same way with God's character, whether or not he was good. This process would be hard at times, but she would allow God to prove himself. And God was faithful. Though the struggle was intense, in the midst of it all, God proved himself time and again. Then, five years later, at the age of twenty-six, Misha was healed. God intervened in her life in a miraculous way, removing the sickness and the pain.

Now thirty-one, she is happily married to a wonderful man, and they have been blessed with two children. The challenges, however, continue. During the birth of their second child, Misha and the baby almost didn't survive the delivery. At one point in the crisis, doctors thought that even if their lives were spared, one or both would be brain damaged. Instead, both were healthy.

Through it all Misha testifies to a renewed sense of God's presence in her life. She boldly agrees with David that "The LORD is gracious and compassionate, slow to anger and rich in love. The LORD is good to all; he has compassion on all he has made" (Ps. 145:8–9). It doesn't mean that she has answers to all her questions. She also doesn't expect to live without pain and suffering. But Misha is eager to affirm that God is good.

As we seek to understand the goodness of God, it is helpful to return to the Garden of Eden, where the relationship between God and man began. Here we see God's original intent. *Eden* means pleasure in the original Hebrew, and the second chapter of Genesis describes the home of humankind as a place of incredible beauty and abundance. It was filled with good things created by God for Adam and Eve to enjoy. From the very beginning, we see that it is God's desire and plan for humankind to experience pleasure, to enjoy life.

Do we really believe that there is nothing more valuable or pleasurable in this life than knowing God?

Moreover, it is important to understand that one aspect of being created in the image of God is that we experience maximum pleasure in the context of our relationship with him. We were created for relationship with him. So, ultimately, Eden was pleasurable for Adam and Eve because God was there with them and they were able to experience an open, unhindered relationship with him.

For us this simply means that we will only experience the fullness of God's goodness if we are in relationship with him. Of course, people can experience a generous measure of God's goodness even without acknowledging him. Atheists are still able to enjoy sunsets and to experience love in relationships, but if God is not acknowledged, then what is ultimately most pleasurable in this life—relationship with God—is unattainable.

The test for all of us comes when we are challenged to question the value of our relationship with God. Do we really believe that there is nothing more valuable or pleasurable in this life than knowing God?

When we walk in obedience, trusting in God, choosing his will, we are most able to enjoy his goodness.

Maybe the most basic form of testing that we encounter is the result of the freedom of choice that God has given us. We are constantly confronted with the choice either to obey or disobey God, to believe or disbelieve. This freedom to choose was presented to us first in the Garden of Eden. In Genesis 2:16–17, God says to man, "You are free to eat from any tree in the garden; but you must not eat from the tree of the knowledge of good and evil." Because we know the end of the story, it may seem that God is merely giving man the opportunity to sin, but it's more than that—God also gives man the opportunity *not* to sin, or rather, the freedom to choose obedience.

As we face this freedom, it is our understanding of the character of God, and especially his goodness, that instructs our choices. If we believe God to be good, we will more easily trust him and more willingly do what he says. As long as Adam and Eve chose to obey God and trust his ways by not eating from the forbidden tree, they walked in the path of blessing and were thus able to enjoy all that God had given them. In the same way, when we walk in obedience, trusting in God, choosing his will, we are most able to enjoy his goodness.

Of course, as we have noted, this path of blessing is not devoid of difficulties. But we need to see each challenge along the path as an opportunity to choose obedience and, in so doing, to express our love for God and embrace his goodness.

It's critical for us to catch a glimpse of what God was doing when he gave us this freedom. God was taking an incredible risk. He made himself vulnerable to us. He took the risk that we might learn to live without him. We might learn self-sufficiency, to live our lives and even to enjoy the good gifts he has given us in his creation while ignoring or even turning our backs on our relationship with him. In this way, the freedom that God has given us is a simple test. Will we take seriously our responsibility to value and maintain our relationship with God? Or will we neglect the relationship and choose to forget God? How are you responding to this test right now in your life?

In the Garden of Eden, we see Adam and Eve choose disobedience. God's goodness is spurned, and their world falls apart. The relationship of trust between God and mankind is violated, and the community between Adam and Eve is broken.

The short passage of Scripture (Gen. 3:1–24) that we refer to as "the Fall" centers on a dialogue between Eve and a serpent (vss. 1–5). The issue in question in this conversation is the goodness of God. The serpent, here being used as an instrument of God's enemy, plants a seed of doubt in Eve's heart. Eve is tempted by the attractive fruit, but at a deeper level she finds herself believing the claim of the serpent, that God is perhaps not as good as she at first believed.

We all struggle with doubt. In fact, honest doubts and questions reveal faith's presence in our hearts, not its absence. But what we do with our doubts is critical. In the example of Eve, we have what *not* to do with doubts. In fact, as soon as she continues in conversation with this deceiver, she falters. She finds herself altering what *God* has said, expanding his command by adding "and you must not touch it" (vs. 3). Then, instead of going to God or to her husband with her doubt, she isolates herself with the serpent and ends up believing his lie. Eve is at odds with her Creator. She thinks she knows what's best. In the end, she sets herself up as her own god, her own ruler. She rejects God's way and chooses her way.

This is, forever, the nature of sin. When we sin, we challenge God's authority and put ourselves on the throne. We disbelieve in God's goodness. We assert that we know what is best for ourselves. Sin is an act of defiance against God. When we sin, we are choosing a pleasure or a course of action of our own design instead of that which God intends for us; we're placing ourselves and our wants above him. Of course, part of the pain of disobedience comes when we realize that we have chosen a *lesser* pleasure or a less fruitful—perhaps even destructive—course of action. We have forfeited what is best.

Why do we sin? Why would we ever choose something less than what is most valuable and, in the end, most pleasurable? Because we do not see things clearly. Our faculties are impaired. Our souls and minds and hearts are completely darkened by a sinful nature. We are diseased, terminally. We are wounded, fatally. We are lost, eternally.

We have only one hope: that God will come looking for us and help us, just as he did with Adam and Eve in the Garden of Eden. After they had sinned, they were hiding from God. In Genesis 3:9 we have one of the most beautiful and amazing verses in the whole Bible: "But the LORD God called to the man, 'Where are you?'" In the same way, wherever our sin has left us, God comes to us and calls out, "Where are you?"

Ultimately, it is in Christ *that we are able to experience all the good that God has intended for us.*

We run away from God, and God runs after us. This is unconditional love. This was the mission of Jesus Christ: "For the Son of Man came to seek and to save what was lost" (Luke 19:10). God wants to draw us to himself and convince us of his great love and goodness. It is his mission to find us and heal us and help us to choose again what is truly good.

Ultimately, it is *in Christ* that we are able to experience all the good that God has intended for us. This is what the apostle Paul has said so emphatically in his letters to the churches. And perhaps in no other letter has he said it better than in his letter to the Ephesians. In the first chapter of that letter he writes, "Long, long ago he decided to adopt us into his family through Jesus Christ" (1:5, MSG). Through this adoption we have the inheritance and all the rights that come from being children of God. We can't even begin to fathom that. Why would God adopt us? He has. It was decided long ago. During Paul's time, in the Roman Empire, an adopted child was chosen by the family and thus had a greater value than a naturally born child. So when Paul says this, he is showing that we have greater value because God specifically chose us.

Just when I think I'm able to grasp his goodness, there is more. In verse 7, Paul says, "Because of the sacrifice of the Messiah…we're a free people—free of penalties and punishments chalked up by all our misdeeds" (MSG). Wow, we are free! How many times have I based my walk with God on what I have done or what I haven't done? So often I've felt like I needed to do penance for my sin because it was just too ugly for the grace of God to cover. But Paul

testifies that we are free from punishment for *all* of
our misdeeds. And that means *all* of them, all of our
sins from years ago, six months ago, yesterday, today,
and for the rest of our lives. We are free. That is good
news.

As Christians we are not primarily in
a religion, or in *a teaching, or* in *a*
state of mind—we are in *a Person.*

Throughout the book of Ephesians, as well as in
his other letters, Paul uses the term *in Christ* over
and over again. What does it mean to be "in Christ"?
It is a description of intimate association. As Christians we are not primarily *in* a religion, or *in* a teaching, or *in* a state of mind—we are *in* a Person. We are
invited to lose ourselves in this relationship. Jesus
said, "If anyone would come after me, he must deny
himself and take up his cross and follow me" (Mark
8:34). Being found "in Christ" requires radical self-
denial and surrender. However, the very next verse
affirms that it is actually in denying ourselves for
Christ that we discover ourselves in Christ: "For whoever wants to save his life will lose it, but whoever

loses his life for me and for the gospel will save it"
(Mark 8:35). When we submit ourselves to Christ's
authority, we are also entrusting ourselves to his
goodness. Jesus commands our obedience but also
promises our ultimate well-being. He calls us to die
to ourselves, that we might live *in him*.

---

*"God, give me a revelation
of who you are today."*

I would encourage you to pick up a newer trans-
lation of the Bible, such as *The Message*, and read
through Ephesians, especially the first two chapters,
with one prayer in mind, "God, show me your goodness." And it is my prayer that God would overwhelm
you with his goodness just as he did with Paul.

When it comes right down to it, what we need
most is a greater revelation of who God is. There is
so much that we don't understand about him and so
much that we misunderstand. In fact, most of the
problems we face in our lives of faith stem from mis-
conceptions about who God is.

After spending many years serving God in
Central Asia, I was for a time back at home in the

United States. During that period, I was struggling within myself over where I should be living and serving God. On the one hand, I was sensing that God was leading me to be in the U.S. for a while. On the other hand, I had this nagging notion that God would be more pleased with me if I were serving him overseas.

My inner turmoil was based on a misunderstanding: I believed that God showed preference toward missionaries and that somehow I could earn his favor simply by moving to another part of the world. I was very wrong, and I had no peace in my heart until God brought clarity to my confusion and affirmed that my worth was not based on where I was serving him.

As we struggle with limitations like this, we must learn to come before God regularly with a simple prayer, "God, give me a revelation of who you are today." We should pray this not only for ourselves but for others as well because nothing else will change our lives more than a deeper knowledge of God. The more we pray this prayer, the more we will desire to experience it. It will become our passion to know God, and the more we know him, the more we will yearn for more of him.

What an amazing journey we are invited to embark on—a relationship with our Creator. What an amazing treasure we have—the opportunity to know God personally. Truly, there is nothing more beautiful, nothing more wonderful, nothing more extravagant that our hearts could desire. This is precisely what the apostle Paul was captivated by when he wrote, "I consider everything a loss compared to the surpassing greatness of knowing Christ Jesus my Lord" (Phil. 3:8).

Is it the cry of your heart to know God? Are you willing right now to lose everything else, as Paul was, in order to gain Christ, in order to go deeper in your relationship with God? If you are unsure about the answers to questions like these, then you have probably allowed other things to cloud your understanding of who God is. But right now God longs to prove himself to you and to bring you to that place of knowing that nothing else is more important than your relationship with him. God longs to captivate your heart. If you are ready and willing to go deeper with God, then brace yourself for the adventure of your life!

It was the author of Hebrews, when writing about faith, who wrote, "For whoever would draw near to God must believe that he exists and *that he rewards those who seek him*" (11:6, RSV, emphasis added). If we are to enjoy and cherish a relationship with God, we must believe in not only God's existence but also his character, that he is good and that he desires to grant us an experience of that goodness.

When we believe this about God, it presents us with the inspiring possibility of trusting him, of giving ourselves wholeheartedly to a relationship with him. It is to this topic, trust, that we will now turn our attention.

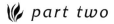 *part two*

Trusting

*God has shown us that he is not only capable of relation-
ship with us but that he is committed to it above all else.
He has given himself to us, and in turn he invites us to give
ourselves to him. This response on our part can generally be
described as* trust. *Just as in any relationship, it requires
something of us, an opening of our hearts. In the following
three chapters I will discuss three aspects of this giving of
ourselves to God: responding to the call to intimacy, dealing with fear, and hearing from God.*

“Come, follow me,” Jesus said.

—*Mark 1:17*

Remain in me, and I will remain in you.

—*Jesus, John 15:4*

chapter three

Intimacy with Jesus

*O*ne day as Jesus was walking beside the Sea of Galilee, he encountered some fishermen. First, he approached two brothers, Simon and Andrew, in the midst of their work. He called out to them, "Come follow me, and I will make you fishers of men." Immediately the two men left their nets and followed him. Next, the same thing happened with another set of brothers, James and John, also working along the shores of the sea.

What would it be like today if Jesus walked into your workplace and did what he did on that day beside the Sea of Galilee? We don't know much about the situation on that day when Jesus met these fishermen, but what we do know is amazing, and it merits some further reflection as we think about God's desire for intimacy with us.

Here are these men at work, fishing, doing what they have always done and probably what their fathers had done before them. They seem to be absorbed in their regular routine when a man walks up to them and invites them to follow him. We don't know if they had ever seen this man before, but apparently, without a question, without any delay, they followed. We may ask about whether or not this was a wise decision, whether or not it was the responsible thing to do. What about their jobs? What about their families? This man told them nothing about the future aside from an obscure promise of transformation, that he would give them a new mission in life and change them into "fishers of men." It seems that, at that point, he offered them nothing more, except himself. And yet they followed.

This call to discipleship was first and foremost an invitation to intimate friendship.

It was the person of Jesus that attracted these fishermen. This call to discipleship was first and foremost an invitation to intimate friendship. Jesus called them to himself—"Come, follow me"—and they obeyed. He was more than just another religious teacher—he was speaking with authority about life and death, and he was offering life itself. The prospect of following this man, of being near to him and receiving from him, was suddenly worth more to them than anything else. These fishermen were captivated by the person of Jesus. His authority compelled them. His love awakened them. His grace energized them.

Is it any different for us today? Jesus hasn't physically walked into our workplace or our school, but he has walked into our lives and called us to be his disciples. He has spoken those same words into our hearts: "Come, follow me." We have been amazed at his unconditional acceptance of us and inspired by his confidence in us. We have been invited into intimate relationship with Jesus, and we have responded to his call.

The lives of the disciples took a radical turn when they encountered Jesus. Some years later, after his death and resurrection, Jesus appeared to a man named Saul, and his life was similarly transformed. He was formerly a zealous member of a group of Jewish teachers called the Pharisees, and he was actively involved in opposing those who followed

Jesus. However, one day, on his way to further harassments, Saul was dramatically confronted by Jesus, who asked him a simple question: "Saul, why are you persecuting me?" Immediately Saul realized the error of his way. The encounter also left him physically blind. But Jesus arranged for a meeting between Saul and a local believer named Ananias. This Ananias prayed for Saul, and Saul experienced both a physical healing and a spiritual rebirth. After further fellowship with local believers, Saul began to take a lead role in proclaiming the gospel of Jesus, and it was not long before he became the prominent leader in the early church, known as the apostle Paul.

Paul's testimony has an important place in the New Testament. It is recounted three times in the book of Acts (in chapters 9, 22, and 26), and it is also reflected upon frequently in Paul's letters to the churches. It was during my imprisonment in Iran that Paul's testimony had a profound impact upon me. I was privileged to have my Bible with me in prison, and I was especially drawn to Paul's letter to the Philippians, a letter he wrote while he was imprisoned for the cause of Christ. One of the resounding themes of that letter is joy and contentment. Paul sums it up near the end of his letter, when he exhorts his readers, "Rejoice in the Lord always. I will say it again: Rejoice!" (4:4).

As I sat in my prison cell, I thought to myself, *How could Paul write so much about rejoicing while sitting in prison?* But the more I read that letter, the more clear it became to me. Paul teaches that a heart that is captivated by Jesus is able to endure any hardship. The joy in Paul's life had nothing to do with his circumstances but everything to do with his relationship with Jesus. At the end of the letter, Paul states that he has learned the secret of contentment (4:12), and we would be sadly amiss if we concluded that it was anything other than the intimacy of his relationship with Jesus. Knowing Jesus was everything to Paul. Everything else was not simply secondary but so secondary that he considered it rubbish (3:8). He was enthralled by the person of Jesus. All of Paul's accomplishments (of which he had many) were rubbish in comparison. All of his hardships and struggles were equally unworthy of distracting him from Jesus. Aside from imprisonment, Paul had suffered a wide variety of tortures, misfortunes, and deprivations (which he lists in 2 Corinthians 11:23–28). All of this faded into insignificance for Paul compared to the value of knowing Jesus. Intimacy with Jesus was his life.

There are many passages of Scripture that have challenged me in the area of intimacy with Jesus but none more than the words of Jesus himself in John 15.

After three years with his disciples, Jesus begins to focus more and more on his departure and to prepare them for life without his physical presence. It would have been very difficult for these dedicated disciples to imagine life without Jesus. How would they survive without him?

I am the vine; you are the branches. If a man remains in me and I in him, he will bear much fruit; apart from me you can do nothing.
—Jesus in John 15:5

Jesus answers this question in John 15. He uses a familiar image, that of a vine, and he invites the disciples to relate this image to their relationship with him. His message is clear: "Remain in me, and I will remain in you. No branch can bear fruit by itself; it must remain in the vine. Neither can you bear fruit unless you remain in me. I am the vine; you are the branches. If a man remains in me and I in him, he will bear much fruit; apart from me you can do nothing" (vss. 4–5).

It's a simple lesson but very profound. Jesus is calling his disciples to intimacy. It involves both an invitation ("remain in me") and a promise ("I will remain in you"). Even after his physical departure, Jesus will be with his followers by the Holy Spirit, and his followers will be with him as they acknowledge his presence. The metaphor helps to define for the disciples how they will continue to follow Jesus after his departure. Their sole responsibility will be to stay connected to the vine, to nurture their relationship with Jesus. Intimacy with him will still be a reality through the Holy Spirit, and as they maintain that intimacy, their lives will reveal the evidence of it—they will bear fruit.

As we consider these truths for our own lives, we need to appreciate the simple fact that fruit grows on branches that are connected to the vine. So often we assume that bearing fruit is, somehow, our own responsibility. We strive to produce the evidence of our faith. We worry about proving to others that we are worthy. We compete and we perform. But all the while we are distracted from the very thing that allows for fruit in our lives—intimacy with Jesus.

Maybe it seems too simple. Maybe it seems too easy. But the truth is, if we remain connected to Jesus, the fruit will happen. In some ways it is a mystery that large luscious fruit appear on skinny dry branches. In the same way it may be surprising to us and to others that beautiful things emerge from our lives. But the source of life is not in the branch itself. It only passes through the branch from the vine. Just as the branch receives its life from the vine, so we receive life from Jesus.

Jesus is all you need. You need only to remain in him and then watch what he will do with your life.

It is humbling to remember that we are branches and not vines. We need Jesus. We can accomplish nothing of lasting value without him, and yet with him we have such incredible potential. I learned this in a new way as I sat in prison for nine weeks in Iran. During that time I came to the end of myself. How could I bear fruit while sitting alone in a prison cell? The answer was simply by abiding in the vine. In my despair and loneliness, I clung to Christ, and now as I look back on that time, I can see how, in many ways, it was the most fruitful time of my life. Not only was God developing my Christian character and deepening my faith and trust in him, he was also using me to draw others to himself, even without my knowing of it. To my amazement, God used me to reveal his love to those around me. Before I left prison, I saw some profound changes in the hearts of the prison guards, the interrogator, and the judge.

The key is that Jesus will cause us to be fruitful. We may have strategies on fruitfulness and formulas and books that tell us how to achieve it. But in the end Jesus is all you need. You need only to remain in him and then watch what he will do with your life.

This posture of trust, of letting the life of Jesus flow through us, brings us deep and lasting joy. In John 15:11 Jesus says, "I have told you this so that my joy may be in you and that your joy may be complete." Jesus invites us to find ultimate joy and satisfaction in him. He is all we need. If we are looking elsewhere for this fulfillment, we are looking in vain. No amount of money can deliver the same kind of joy. No other relationship, no job, no drug—nothing— can give us joy like Jesus himself can.

There is a small book that has had a great influence upon me and many others in helping to understand the life of abiding in Christ in practical terms. It is called *The Practice of the Presence of God,* written by Brother Lawrence, a seventeenth-century monk. Brother Lawrence tells of his simple life in the monastery, where among other things he carried out daily duties in the kitchen. It was his goal to continually acknowledge God's presence with him. In the midst of whatever he was doing, he would maintain a silent and secret conversation with God. It was not an easy task, but Brother Lawrence persevered. And just as Jesus promised in John 15:11, this devout monk also experienced the joy of abiding in Christ. He wrote, "There is not in the world a kind of life more sweet and delightful than that of a continual conversation with God. Those only can comprehend it who practice and experience it."[1]

One of the practical things we must do in order to abide in Christ is to seek to keep our whole lives centered on him. This involves a daily challenge to prioritize our activities. From a young age, I learned to meet this challenge with what I call a "list approach" to priorities. I would simply make a list of the things that were most important in my life, something like this:

1. God
2. Family
3. Ministry
4. Friends
5. Recreation

Whether or not I wrote them down, I made these lists all the time and tried to order my day according to them. Sometimes I succeeded at this, and sometimes I did not.

We need to think of God as the sun in our lives. He is at the center and his light shines into every part of our lives.

As I have walked with the Lord now for many years, I have found some serious problems with this way of prioritizing. For example, it seems to me that when we involve ourselves with any of the priorities other than the first, which is God, we tend to leave God behind. We begin to view certain daily activities as secular, and so we don't invite God to be a part of them. Conversely, we think of other things as sacred, such as Bible reading and prayer, and we can find ourselves doing those things out of a performance orientation, thinking we can actually secure God's love for us by doing them. I also have found that when I prioritize this way, I am not allowing God to be in control. Instead I'm trying to run my own life and only fitting in God where I can, or where I really feel I need to. I don't allow for God's timing in things, and so I miss out on experiencing the freedom in following his leading. We may give God some time first thing in the morning as we rush through a few Bible verses and say a few quick prayers, but often we then find it easy to leave God out of our lives for the rest of the day. This is certainly not the kind of approach that was modeled by Jesus or by his disciples.

Everything we do needs to be influenced by our center, our relationship with God.

I now prefer another priority system, one that I simply call a centering approach. This is where Jesus is at the center and everything flows out from my relationship with him. Think about our solar system, with the sun as its center. Everything revolves around the sun and is affected in some way by the light of the sun. We need to think of God as the sun in our lives. He is at the center, and his light shines into every part of our lives. This approach acknowledges that everything in our lives needs to be affected by God's presence. Nothing is outside of his eager interest. And as we submit our whole selves to him, nothing we do is outside of his influence. This is what I believe Jesus modeled for us, which he affirmed in statements like, "I do nothing on my own" (John 8:28; see also 5:30). He was always listening for the voice of the Father and paying attention to what God was doing in each and every situation. In the same way, everything we do needs to be influenced by our center, our relationship with God. We always need to be conscious of our Lord and his priorities, his desires. This way Jesus is involved in everything we do.

How do we decide what is right to do during the day? If God says that we need to spend time with this friend for the next couple of hours, then we should do it wholeheartedly, not feeling that we are neglecting our families or our other friends. Or what if we have peace about going to a movie with a friend? Is that somehow less spiritual than spending time in personal devotions? Of course not! If we have a sense that God is leading us, then we need not worry about the other priority. Now, is it better to pray for two hours or to do something else? Neither is better! The question is rather one of obedience. This is true freedom. It's best to do what we feel Jesus is leading us to do. That is best! Nothing else!

The more Jesus rules and reigns in our lives, the more freedom we experience.

Not all Christians are familiar with this kind of intimate interaction with Jesus. Until they discover that this can be a reality for them, the list approach functions as a viable option. But if intimacy with Jesus is possible, then the centering approach becomes the more exciting way to live out that relationship.

Who better to run our lives than the one who made us and loves us? Jesus wants the best for us.

However, other Christians *prefer* to live by the list approach because, in fact, they are happy to leave God out of most of their lives, even if they regularly give him some of their time. In other words, they want to run their own lives. They want to be in charge of their jobs, their money, and their free time. How sad this is! It only shows a lack of understanding of who Jesus is. Really, the more we know him, the more we will want to have him ruling our lives. Who better to run our lives than the one who made us and loves us? Jesus wants the best for us. But many people have closed God out of their lives because they fear that he will tell them to do something they don't want to do, or that he will ask them to give up something they don't want to give up.

I remember when I first arrived at Wheaton College in 1985. I had looked for a Christian college where I could pursue my studies and also grow in my faith through chapels and Christian fellowship. During my first weeks there, however, things did not go as I had planned. It was much more challenging academically than I had expected. Friendships were very hard for me to make, and the chapels, in my opinion, were boring. In short, I hated it at Wheaton.

Then, in the third week, things got even worse. During a football game, I broke my arm in four places and was hospitalized for five days. As I returned to campus with a clumsy cast on my arm, I vented my frustrations to God, "What in the world is going on? I came here for all the right reasons, but it's all been going wrong!"

It was there in my deep aggravation that God met me. It was there that I heard him ask me a simple question: *Dan, what is the most important thing in your life?*

To that I answered, "You are, and my relationship with you."

Then he challenged me again: *Dan, is your relationship with me really more important than anything else?*

This time I paused, and after some thought I could only say, "It's supposed to be." At that point I realized that my relationship with God wasn't everything to me. If it had been, then the trials I was experiencing at school would not have affected me in the same way. The next day I repented and asked Jesus to captivate my heart once again.

During the next two weeks, he answered that prayer and more. I experienced a complete transformation. Not only did I begin to love being at Wheaton and to make friends more easily, but I had learned more about what Jesus described in the Beatitudes: "You're blessed when you feel you've lost what is most dear to you. Only then can you be embraced by the One most dear to you" (Matt. 5:4, MSG).

As I have taught on the topic of centering our lives on Jesus, one issue that frequently comes up is how this approach relates to our times of quiet devotion and prayer. This question has challenged me to think quite differently about personal devotional time. Setting aside time for personal devotions has been a very significant part of my Christian life, but sometimes I have made the mistake of using that time as an excuse to neglect prayer throughout the rest of my day. We don't just enter God's presence during our personal devotions; he is always with us. We need to appreciate times of solitude, but we also need to learn, like Brother Lawrence, to practice his presence throughout the day, no matter what tasks we are involved in. Our personal devotions are only part of each entire day spent with Jesus.

I am also often asked about how the centering approach relates to raising children. During my childhood I often heard it implied that ministry needs to come before everything else, including family. More recently the emphasis seems to have switched, placing family ahead of ministry.

In my mind, we need to have a God-centered focus on *both* ministry and family, but since I don't have children, I have asked my friends and family members who are parents how they have dealt with this issue. I have received a variety of answers. Both my sisters and their husbands have been serving God in India for many years, and they have raised their children in that context. They have remained faithful to both ministry and family, not only by entrusting their children into the loving care of their heavenly Father, but also by allowing those children to be involved in the ministry themselves. Instead of ranking these priorities, they have worked at maintaining a healthy interaction between ministry and family.

I once asked Loren Cunningham, the founder of Youth With A Mission, for his perspective on this. Somewhat puzzled, he answered simply, "It's not about ministry or even about family, it's just about God. It's about doing the next thing God has told you to do." When his two kids graduated from high school, they honored their parents publicly for centering their lives on God. I hope I can live this model out when I have a family of my own.

The centering approach develops a wholehearted reliance on Jesus. It forces us to always go back to him.

When we begin to live more and more by a centering approach, it brings up the obvious question, How do I know what the Lord wants? Later (in chapter 5) we will discuss the issue of hearing God's voice, but here it may be enough to say that it is not always easy to know what the Lord wants. He doesn't necessarily tell us in each and every situation. Sometimes discerning the will of God in a particular situation is a process.

Whatever the challenge, we need to remember that God is most concerned about the condition of our hearts, that they are fully submitted to him and centered on him. When we keep asking the question, "Lord, what do you want?" it helps us to stay focused. We only need to be sure that we are ready and willing to obey when he does make known his will to us.

In this way the centering approach develops a wholehearted reliance on Jesus. It forces us to always go back to him, and that is precisely what he wants. Frequently running to him to find out the next thing to do can often be a struggle, but I have learned to see the struggle as a gift because the struggle pushes us to prayer and into further depending on him. It deepens the relationship between us and God. Again, this is exactly what Jesus wants. Intimacy is his desire.

In some ways a centering approach is very difficult. It requires more from us than prioritizing and the giving of parts of our lives to God—it demands *everything.* But its demands are far outweighed by the joy it brings by helping us stay connected to Jesus and reliant on him in the whole of our lives. It helps me to understand what happened at the Sea of Galilee when Jesus called the first disciples. Those disciples realized what Jesus was requiring of them. They didn't just rearrange their priorities, they gave up everything to follow him.

The more you center your mind and heart on Jesus, the more you will have his mind and his heart for the situations you encounter throughout your day.

It seems to me that this is similar to what the apostle Paul had in mind when he challenged the Colossian believers, writing, "Since, then, you have been raised with Christ, set your hearts on things above, where Christ is seated at the right hand of God. Set your minds on things above, not on earthly things" (3:1–2). The more you center your mind and heart on Jesus, the more you will have his mind and his heart for the situations you encounter throughout your day.

I love how Loren Cunningham talks about the life that is centered on Jesus. "I want to lean so hard on Jesus that if he moved, I would fall down." That's a beautiful way! I want to be so dependent on Jesus that if he moved, I'd have to move as well. I'd fall over without him at my side. It's similar to Peter's response when Jesus asked if the disciples would abandon him as others had done. Peter said, "Lord, to whom shall we go? You have the words of eternal life" (John 6:68). Indeed, we are completely lost without Jesus at our side.

It has often been said that the last words Jesus spoke to his disciples before he ascended into heaven are of supreme importance. The command of Jesus to "go and make disciples of all nations" (Matt. 28:19) has deeply inspired me to invest my life in serving others. It has challenged me to be willing to do anything and go anywhere for Jesus. But something that has impacted me almost as much is what Jesus *didn't* say upon his departure. He didn't tell his followers a lot about *how* to fulfill their mission. He didn't present them with a long list of tasks and responsibilities. It's amazing to think about how little he actually left with those disciples. How would they have felt? I would think that they probably felt quite overwhelmed with the idea of continuing what Jesus had begun. It probably seemed almost laughable, as they looked around at one another, that they were the chosen ones to see the kingdom of God come to earth.

*We don't have a formula, a guaranteed
strategy, or a how-to manual. We have
what the disciples had—Jesus himself.
What could be better than that?*

For these simple men, the sweetest of Jesus' parting words must have been the very last, as recorded in the Gospel of Matthew, "And surely I am with you always, to the very end of the age" (Matt. 28:20). In the midst of all their questions and potential confusion, these words must have sounded beautifully reassuring. The disciples didn't need a formula or a detailed how-to manual. They needed Jesus, and that is what they got. Jesus promised them himself, his continued presence with them. He invited them to a relationship with him that they would continue to nurture by faith. He said, "I am with you."

Jesus would have us hear the same words today. Just as the disciples were left with a daunting task and a simple promise, so we have the same task and the same wonderful promise. Jesus will be with us as we each go into "all the world," whether that means going into the classroom, the workplace, the house next door, or around the globe. We don't have a formula, a guaranteed strategy, or a how-to manual. We have what the disciples had—Jesus himself. What could be better than that?

Jesus called the disciples, and he calls us, to run to him all day long with everything. He is with us. We have relationship with him. Words cannot express how amazing this reality is. If you receive anything from this book, receive this: Jesus is with you and longs for relationship with you. This is what life is all about.

1. Brother Lawrence, *The Practice of the Presence of God,* (New Kensington, Penn.: Whitaker House, 1982), p. 29.

❦ There is no fear in love. But perfect love drives out fear.

—*1 John 4:18*

❦ For God has not given us a spirit of fear and timidity, but of power, love, and self-discipline.

—*2 Timothy 1:7* (NLT)

chapter four

Dealing with Fear

*T*he fact that Jesus is always with us wherever we go doesn't mean that we don't encounter fear as we follow him. On the contrary, the life of faith is filled with risk and uncertainty. There is often much to fear, and it is quite natural and normal for us to be afraid. However, in the very midst of this, Jesus calls out to us and says, "Do not be afraid." It is not as much a command as it is an invitation to face those fears and to trust in him. It is in the loving embrace of Jesus that we experience perfect love and find the courage and strength to overcome that which makes us afraid.

The apostle Peter was a man of great zeal and emotion. One stormy night he and some of the other disciples were out on a boat in the Sea of Galilee. (See Matt. 14:22–33.) In the midst of the storm, Jesus appeared and approached them, walking on the water. The disciples didn't recognize him, so they were terrified until Jesus spoke to them, "Take courage! It is I. Don't be afraid." At that moment, Peter spoke up boldly and said, "Lord, if it's you, tell me to come to you on the water." Peter was willing to step out. He was willing to face his fears and to take the risk of faith.

Jesus responded to his challenge and said, "Come." I love how Jesus dealt with Peter. He saw his faith and rewarded him, though I'm sure the other disciples couldn't help but roll their eyes as they listened to Peter's latest outburst.

I want to simply obey. I want to step out in faith and walk on water.

So what did Peter do? He got out of the boat and walked on the water toward Jesus. Peter experienced a miracle! So often when we hear this story, we focus on what happened next, when Peter took his eyes off of Jesus and began to sink. But we need to appreciate what happened before that—Peter walked on water!

What would that have been like for Peter? Was he at all hesitant as he stepped out of the boat? Did he touch the water with one foot first to test it out? What would *you* have done? I probably would have said, "Sure, Lord, I'd love to come to you on the water. Just provide a way, maybe another boat, or maybe you could part the lake like you parted the Red Sea for Moses. You make a way and I will come."

All that seems to have mattered for Peter was the invitation that Jesus gave him: "Come." Everything else at that point became unimportant. Whatever else was going on around him and within him, he was able simply to focus on God and walk toward the open arms of Jesus. In many ways it doesn't matter that Peter's faith wavered moments later. He was already closer to the arms of Jesus than any of the other disciples. And when he did begin to sink, Jesus was there to catch him. Peter was the only one who experienced the miracle; the others only witnessed it.

I don't know about you, but I want to be like Peter. No matter what Jesus asks me to do, I want to step out in faith. No matter what others may think. No matter how crazy or impossible it may look. I want to simply obey. I want to step out in faith and walk on water.

The remedy for every fear is the same: a deeper trust in God and a growing confidence that he will care for us and help us through any challenge that we face.

Sadly, our fears often keep us from stepping out in faith and obeying God. As I travel and teach, I hear many Christians, young and old, talk about their fears. Ten common fears that I have come across are:

1. The fear of loneliness
2. The fear of man
3. The fear of death
4. The fear of rejection
5. The fear of being misunderstood
6. The fear of pain
7. The fear of not having financial security
8. The fear of failure
9. The fear of missing God's will
10. The fear of the unknown or of change

These are all fears that I have personally experienced and continue to face. Many who know about my international adventures have come to me and said, "Dan, you are so courageous to have done all that you have done." But those who know me better know about my many struggles with fear. I'm sure that as you read a list like the one above you are able to identify the fears that plague you as well.

In some ways I wish I could offer a simple way to do away with fears, but I cannot. I can only testify to the fact that God has helped me to overcome many and various fears, and I am increasingly experiencing God's victory over fear. I assure you that God can help you in the same way.

Though I will not deal here with each of the listed fears individually, I want to deal with fear in general by offering examples from my own experience.

There is no fear that can keep
us from obeying God.

First, it is evident that these fears tend to overlap, and often it is difficult to understand the nature of the fear that we are experiencing. However, the remedy for every fear is the same: a deeper trust in God and a growing confidence that he will care for us and help us through any challenge that we face. We need to realize that there is no fear that can keep us from obeying God. Fear can never become an excuse to run away from God. If anything, fear should drive us into the arms of God.

One of the most difficult personal struggles I have encountered has been the fear of being alone, and specifically the fear of never getting married. I remember sitting in the church at my younger sister's wedding and thinking about the fact that Christina was four years younger than I and yet married before me. God had provided for her but why not for me? I struggled with discouragement. I've also watched most of my friends get married and have children, and I've asked the Lord whether or not I would ever get married myself. I don't feel that God has spoken much to me on the issue.

As this fear surfaces and even as depression sometimes sets in, I have learned to run to God and to surrender it to him. Who is able to meet my deepest social and emotional needs? Jesus alone. Whether we are single or married, if we don't believe that he is enough, then we grasp for satisfaction in other things. There is so much more to know about Jesus, so much more to experience. I have told myself again and again that ultimately Jesus is all I need. To be honest, sometimes even though I know that is true, and maybe it is the right thing to say, I struggle to really believe it. Every time we feel that he isn't enough, we need to ask God to reveal more of who he is. He will be faithful to answer that prayer and to increase our understanding of who he is and of his ability to meet all of our needs.

Our fears are dealt with in the context of relationship. We are invited to trust in our heavenly Father and watch our fears be dethroned by his intimate love.

I know that many have battled with this fear and that it has caused many of us to be hesitant about fulfilling what God has called us to do. This can be especially true when that calling will take us overseas. When I first went to Afghanistan, I knew that my prospects of getting married out there were slim, and sometimes that reality frustrated me. I needed to be reminded again and again that Jesus knows our needs. He knows our deepest desires. He wants to meet each of us where we are and take care of all our needs. He is completely trustworthy.

In Romans 8:15 Paul writes, "For you did not receive a spirit that makes you a slave again to fear, but you received the Spirit of sonship. And by him we cry '*Abba*, Father.'" This wonderful truth affirms again that our fears, including the fear of being alone, are dealt with in the context of relationship. As children of God we are invited to trust in our heavenly Father and watch our fears be dethroned by his intimate love.

I am amazed as I watch my nephews and nieces grow up, and I have been especially struck by the trust they have in their parents. I have a vivid memory of one of my nephews jumping off a table into the arms of my brother-in-law. He trusted his father and had complete confidence that he would catch him. God desires that each one of us would test him in the same way. He is completely trustworthy as we step out in faith.

Another fear I have often encountered is the fear of man. One of the most intense and trying times during my imprisonment in Iran was when I was put on trial. Facing two death sentences, I was brought into a courthouse to make them official. I was led before the judge and told to take my place on the witness stand. The judge looked at me intently and said, "Mr. Baumann, tell us why you came to Iran."

I took a long pause as I considered what to say. The judge waited for my answer. The video cameras also waited. I was scared and intimidated as the fear of man gripped me. But as I thought and prayed, I knew I had to be honest. There was no substitute for my integrity. I knew that they might kill me if I answered honestly, but I had to tell the truth about why I came to Iran.

As I opened my mouth to speak, something stronger than fear rose up within me. The Spirit of God was giving me courage and confidence. I looked directly at the judge and said, "I came to Iran to tell people like you about Jesus Christ."

I would like to say that those words came easy, but the truth is I struggled to speak and I was much afraid. But God gave me the grace to proclaim my faith despite my fears. He gave me strength to share my heart and to testify about Jesus. The more I shared, the stronger and bolder I became and the less my fears beset me.

The growing freedom that I experienced as I stood before that judge was indescribable. He had the power to order my execution right then and there, and yet I knew that even death could not separate me from God. If this was to be my time to leave this earth, then I was ready. On that day in the Iranian courtroom, I realized I was free. My fear had been overcome.

More recently, early in 2001, I was given the opportunity to visit Baghdad, Iraq. The Ministry of Religion in Iraq had extended an invitation to Christian leaders from around the world to come visit the country, view the effects of foreign sanctions, and assess the humanitarian needs. A friend of mine invited me to accompany him on this tour. I saw it as a unique opportunity to visit this needy country. As I prayed about the trip, I felt a peace about going and sensed that it would be a significant time for me.

Despite this initial confidence in prayer, as the date of departure came closer, the fear of man again surfaced in my heart. I was reminded of some of the details of my imprisonment in Iran. I feared that the Iraqi authorities could do to me what the Iranian authorities had done in the past. During the weeks leading up to the trip, on more than one occasion, I seriously considered backing out. But I knew that the Lord wanted to bring me to a deeper level of trust in him. I knew that I needed to walk through this situation and allow my faith to be tested.

In May 2001 my friend and I headed to Jordan, where we picked up our visas and boarded a bus headed for Baghdad. Despite my fears, Jesus met me at every step of the way. As I walked by faith, the fears had less and less of a hold on me. It was a fabulous journey. We had a wonderful time interacting with the Iraqi people and visiting the ancient cities of Babylon, Ur, and Nineveh. My love for Iraq and its people grew strong, and as I left, I was so thankful that Jesus had not only given me that opportunity to go, but that he had given me the courage to face my fear.

Sometimes fear arises in our hearts when our obedience has the potential to affect others negatively, when it brings others into a place where *they* are vulnerable to pain or injury. I faced this kind of difficulty when I returned home after my time in prison in Iran. I was approached by a group of Iranian Christians who seriously questioned my decision to ever enter Iran. They reprimanded me for putting the national believers at risk. Indeed, some of the believers that we contacted in Iran had subsequently been questioned and imprisoned themselves. This was incredibly difficult for me. I struggled within myself, trying to reconcile the confidence we felt about going into Iran with the trouble it had caused.

The very people in Iran that we had sought out to love had been hurt in the wake of our visit. Had God really called us into Iran? As I wrestled with this, I recalled how confident we were that God had led us to make the trip for the purpose of exploring future service opportunities. I knew in my heart that, as far as we were concerned, we had done what Jesus had asked us to do. We had trusted and obeyed.

*It is important to be aware of risk,
but as Christians we shouldn't
base our decisions on it.*

A few months later, after this initial turmoil, I received some very encouraging words from Loren Cunningham. He affirmed that there is honor in doing what God has asked us to do, whatever the consequences for ourselves and others. We must leave the results of our obedience in God's hands. Of course we need to give serious consideration to how our actions will affect others, but we also must trust God that what he asks us to do will, in the end, be the best for all those involved. Again, our responsibility is to trust and obey. Yes, we need to be sure of our guidance, but in the same way that we entrust our-selves into God's hands, we also need to entrust the lives of others into his hands.

The more we step out to trust in God, the more we will be confronted with decisions that involve some element of risk. In Western society today, we avoid risk at all costs. We have made a god out of security and safety. When we must take a risk, we are encouraged to carefully calculate it and to methodi-cally minimize it. There is some wisdom in this, but we have taken it to an extreme. It is important to be aware of risk, but as Christians we shouldn't base our decisions on it.

Risk comes not only to the person heading out into potentially dangerous situations but also to those who care about them. Parents, for instance, take a risk in releasing their children to follow their own callings. Even though I don't have children, I know that it can be a considerable challenge—and a high calling—for parents to trust God with their chil-dren's lives. I admire my own parents for how they have released all three of us to the purposes of God. Each of us has lived in Asia for many years and faced a variety of hardships. Elisabeth, my older sister, has lived in India and Nepal for the past twenty-two years and was once imprisoned in Nepal. I was imprisoned in Iran and before that spent many years in the war-torn country of Afghanistan. My younger sister, Christina, lived for years in India's northernmost state, Kashmir, considered by the U.S. State Department to be one of the most unsafe places in the world. Were my parents crazy to let us live in such risky and unsafe environments? They would say no. In fact, my parents have considered it an honor to release their kids to Jesus in this way. The more they trust in him, the more they realize that he is trustworthy.

The safest place in the world is in the center of God's will.

I remember hearing about the first public prayer meeting that my mother attended after she received the news of my imprisonment in Iran. She prayed, with great boldness and courage, "Lord, I ask that Dan would not be released from prison until all of your purposes are fulfilled." Mom is intense. What kind of a mother would pray that kind of a prayer? One who is totally trusting her son into the care of her heavenly Father. One who has had a glimpse of eternity and longs for God's eternal purposes to be fulfilled in her own life and in the lives of her children. I'm glad, though, that there were others praying for my quick release!

Ultimately we have nothing to fear. Jesus loves us, and he invites us to be confident in that love. As we seek to obey him, we are not called to assess the risk involved and determine whether or not obedience will be beneficial or safe for us. We are simply called to trust and obey.

So often, even as Christians, we try to assess situations according to our own limited notions of safety. We are consumed by this. It's such a priority for us. We will not do certain things just because of the risk involved. In the face of this kind of thinking, we need to affirm that the safest place in the world is in the center of God's will. If God really does care for me, then this is what I must believe. According to some, I have made many *unsafe* decisions in my lifetime, but never have I regretted trusting in God. I have made my home in different war zones. I have been held at gunpoint. I have endured imprisonment. But in the midst of it all, despite many fears, I have known the goodness of the Lord, and my confidence in him has only been strengthened.

Some may wonder how I came to the place where I was so confident with these big decisions. The only answer I can give is that this kind of trust is a natural outcome of everyday relationship with God, living out the centered approach (as discussed in chapter 3). As you get to know God more intimately, you know that you can trust him with everything.

---

*Seek first his kingdom and his
righteousness, and all these things
will be given to you as well.*
—*Matthew 6:33*

One of the things that I have learned over the years is that there are no big and small decisions in trusting God. Whether we are trusting him with which movie to watch, which house to buy, what to do on our days off, or what to do as we travel overseas, it's all the same. Everything is about trusting God.

God calls each one of us to take risks, to make ourselves vulnerable in a variety of ways. When God asks you to do something that seems risky or unsafe, go to him in prayer. Bring your fears and anxieties before Jesus. He will take care of you. Don't allow those fears or the feelings of being unsafe to determine your decisions. Simply trust and obey.

Risks to our physical safety are not the only challenges we may face. Sometimes God asks us to take financial risks. Just as we may make decisions based on what we think is financially prudent or possible, we may hesitate to obey God until we know we have sufficient funds to cover our costs. But the words of Jesus are always challenging in this regard: "Seek first his kingdom and his righteousness, and all these things will be given to you as well" (Matt. 6:33). Jesus is committed to taking care of us. He will provide for us.

Those serving with YWAM have many stories to share about God's financial provision. I had the privilege of being very close to one of those stories. I was attending a discipleship program in Holland. One of the girls in our school, Alisha, felt that God wanted her to join the program's outreach team going to Hong Kong. She needed about US$1200 to cover her costs. After many weeks of praying and asking God to provide, Alisha had only $250, so she gave up on the idea of going on the outreach. The day came for her team to leave, and with many tears and frustrations, she went to the airport to see them off and say her goodbyes. While she was at the airport, a woman she didn't know walked up to her and asked, "Are you with YWAM?"

When Alisha said she was, the woman continued, "Well, last night I was awakened by the Lord, and he told me to come here today to the airport and to give you this." The woman gave Alisha one thousand dollars. She couldn't believe it! She had a wonderful outreach in Hong Kong. Oh, that we would have the grace not to let money stand in the way of doing what God has called us to do.

Sometimes we give in to fears and miss the opportunity that God is giving us at the moment. I have done this many times. On one occasion, six months after my release from prison in Iran, I was given the opportunity to return to Afghanistan. For many reasons I had a deep sense of peace that God was leading me back to Kabul, in part to help me face my fears about returning to that area of the world. I had invited a friend of mine, Chad, to come with me on the trip. At that time the only way into the country was overland from Peshawar, Pakistan. After arriving in Pakistan, we realized that it would take a couple of days to complete the paperwork necessary to enter Afghanistan. As the day approached, fear gripped my heart. It became overwhelming for me, and on the day before we were to leave, I decided that I would not go. It wasn't a decision I made in prayer. It wasn't that I sensed God had changed my plan. I simply gave in to my fears.

My friend Chad decided to go alone, and as I hugged him goodbye early that next morning, my heart was filled with shame. Not only had I disobeyed God, but I had let down my friend, whom I had planned to host in a country I loved. God, however, was gracious. Even while I was still in Peshawar waiting for Chad to return, the Lord began to encourage me and to show me the many other wonderful things he had in store for me, but all I wanted to do was grovel in my failures for a while. But Jesus, wonderful Jesus, had other plans. He wanted to lift up my head and lead me on. He was eager to give me another chance. Somehow my failure didn't exhaust his grace. The failure just opened up another opportunity. Six months later God opened the door again, and I had the privilege of returning to Kabul, where I spent two wonderful months.

Despite such testimonies to God's grace, we often still struggle with a fear of failure. I've learned a lot about God's perspective on our failures as I've thought about how children learn to walk. I watched carefully as my nephew Caleb took his first step and fell to the floor. How did his father respond? Did he say, "Oh well, son, you tried, but you failed. Sorry, I guess you can't walk. You had your chance, but you blew it"? Of course not! That would be ludicrous. But often this is how we think God responds to our failures. Caleb's father doesn't focus on the fall, he focuses on the step: "Look, my son is walking!" God is the same with us. He doesn't focus on our failures. Like a loving father, he is eager to pick us up when we fall and is excited for us to try again.

Learning to trust in God is a process, and along the journey we begin to understand more and more about his character.

Learning to trust in God is a process, and along the journey we begin to understand more and more about his character, enabling us to trust him more. As we walk out this adventure with God, our lives are filled with opportunities to take steps of faith, often requiring us to face the uncertain and the unknown.

In 1989, while I was working in Afghanistan, the Soviet forces withdrew from the country. Due to the civil unrest that followed, all the foreign workers were encouraged to evacuate. I went to Thailand for a few weeks to decide what I would do next. While there I asked the Lord to speak to me about what he wanted me to do for the next couple of months. I felt that he spoke to me about going to the northwestern part of

China to spend a few weeks praying for the Uyghur people. (The Uyghurs are a Turkic Muslim people numbering about ten million and considered to be unreached with the gospel.) After wrestling with God about this for a while, I finally decided that I would have to obey him. So I secured a visa for China, then went to a YWAM training center nearby to ask if anyone there knew someone in the Uyghur area of northwest China. One man that I talked with said, "Yes, I think there's a man named Mike Brown from Australia who is a friend of YWAM and is studying the language up there, somewhere in the province."

I thought to myself, *I need more than this to go on.* The next day I brought my concerns to the Lord, praying, "Lord, I need more specifics. I need a contact up there. This Mike might be up there somewhere, but that province has a population of over twenty-five million people. I need someone with a specific address." Again heaven was silent.

After a few days, still with very little to go on, I left for China. I arrived in Beijing, uncertain and afraid, thinking to myself, *Why did I ever allow myself to come here?* I walked out of the airport and saw two young Japanese men standing at a tourist center. I hadn't yet found anyone who spoke English, so I approached them and asked, "Do you speak English?"

"A little," they replied.

Without hesitation I blurted out, "I want to stay with you tonight." They looked at each other briefly and agreed. At least I had someone I could talk to.

My plan was to go to the train station in the morning and book a ticket on the next train leaving for the city of Urumchi in the northwest. When I came to the counter and told the woman there what I wanted, she replied, "The next train for Urumchi leaves in four days."

"What?!" I blurted out. "But I need to go tomorrow."

I did not have the money to stay longer in Beijing, and besides, I hadn't come to China to visit Beijing. And surely my new Japanese friends didn't expect me to stay with them that long. But apparently I had no choice. As I began to walk away from the counter, the woman called out to me, "Sir, by the way, the train ride to Urumchi lasts ninety-two hours."

I stopped, turned around, and said, "Ninety-two hours?"

The woman smiled and said, "Yes, sir."

Four days later I said goodbye to my Japanese friends and boarded the train for Urumchi. After ninety-two hours I arrived in the city at 6 a.m. and was greeted with subzero temperatures. I had met one Chinese person on the train who spoke some English. He told me about the many universities and other institutions in the city of two million people and offered to take me to the largest university and drop me at the front gate.

Soon I stood at that gate, freezing. It was still dark outside, and the city seemed very barren. As I stood there, hopelessness began to set in. What in the world was I thinking back there in Thailand? There is no way that I will find this Mike Brown. Why did I allow myself to come here? God would have forgiven me if I had disobeyed, but at least I wouldn't have been in this mess. In my desperation, I turned my head toward the sky and cried out to Jesus, "Lord, I need you. I have no idea what to do."

Immediately, as clearly as I have ever heard the Lord, he spoke to my heart. *Dan, walk to the center of the campus.* I did. *Now make a right turn and walk down this pathway until you reach that big building.* Once I got to the building, I heard him say, *Now go inside and stand in the corridor for twenty minutes.*

By now I was beginning to question this whole escapade more and more. I thought to myself that I must be losing it. It was crazy. As I stood there, many students walked by me and stared at me, and I stared at them. After twenty minutes, God spoke again,

Now walk to the end of this hallway and knock at the last door on the left.

As I was walking, I saw a man come in from a hallway ahead of me and begin walking in the same direction. He went into the last room on the left. I arrived at the room and knocked. As he opened the door, I couldn't believe my eyes. He was another foreigner, a German studying at the university. He invited me in, and we began to speak in English. Then I asked him if he had ever heard of a man from Australia named Mike Brown who was studying the local language somewhere in this province.

He replied, "Yes, Mike is a good friend of mine. He lives right here in the city and is studying at another university. I can take you right to his room." I sat there stunned. Then tears began to well up in my eyes. All the anxiety and fear that I had up until that moment was quickly fading away. Jesus, wonderful Jesus, had come through again. This was one of the greatest miracles I had ever experienced. If I had disobeyed back in Bangkok, I would have totally missed out on this moment. As my eyes turned to heaven, I could see Jesus with a big grin on his face looking down on me and saying, *My son, I love you. Thanks for coming here.*

Minutes later I was sitting with Mike Brown. We talked for hours. I told him the story of how I found him, and we marveled together at the goodness and faithfulness of God. Mike invited me to spend the next few days with him and then arranged for me to be hosted by some friends of his in another part of the province about five hundred miles away. I cherished my time among the Uyghur people, spending much of those three weeks praying for them. Afterward I returned to Beijing and then back to Thailand. What an adventure with Jesus! Oh, the beauty of learning to trust in him.

Are you trusting in God,
or do fears rule your life?

Are you trusting in God, or do fears rule your life? Whatever it is that you are afraid of, Jesus is inviting you now to face that fear and to trust in him. Remember, it is the presence of his perfect love in our hearts that will give us the courage and strength to overcome our fears.

🕯 The LORD came and stood there, calling as at the other times, "Samuel! Samuel!"

Then Samuel said, "Speak, for your servant is listening."

—1 Samuel 3:10

🕯 My sheep listen to my voice;
I know them, and they follow me.

—Jesus, John 10:27

chapter five

Hearing from God

C ommunication is vital in any relationship. Our capacity to hear God's voice is an essential part of our relationship with him. As we open the Scriptures, we encounter a God who speaks. In the very first chapter of Genesis, it is recorded that God *spoke* the world into existence: "And God said, 'Let there be light,' and there was light" (1:3). And as soon as Adam and Eve were created, God interacted with them in a conversational manner—both God and man were able to speak and be spoken to. We see the same kind of thing throughout the Scriptures— God's people hear God's voice. God is intensely interested in individuals, and he desires to communicate in intimate ways with each and every person.

In all of my travels, including a wide variety of speaking engagements, I have found there to be more interest in the topic of hearing God's voice than in any other topic. It is a critical issue among Christians today, especially young people. The church is crying out for understanding and clarity on this topic.

Hearing from God is relational, not mechanical.... Jesus invites each one of us to spend time with him and to become familiar with his voice.

In some ways, however, this subject is daunting. It seems that when it is addressed, it often raises more questions than it offers answers. If the topic of hearing God's voice has been a point of frustration and confusion for you, I would encourage you to focus your attention on God and allow him to give you fresh insight and inspiration on this matter. Rather than seek answers to questions, we need to be refreshed in our faith.

First, we should not be looking for some formula on the topic of hearing God. There aren't three easy steps to figure this out, even though sometimes it seems that's exactly what we want. Hearing from God is relational, not mechanical. It is very much related to trusting and following, as John 10:27 affirms: "My sheep listen to my voice; I know them, and *they follow me*" (emphasis added). In that passage Jesus uses the metaphor of sheep and their shepherd to stress that the capacity to listen comes quite naturally as we spend more and more time with Jesus. Sheep know the voice of their shepherd so well because they hear it all the time. They know the voice because they know the shepherd. Jesus invites each one of us to spend time with him and to become familiar with his voice.

God speaks to us for different reasons, sometimes to affirm us, sometimes to convict us or correct us, and sometimes for some other purpose. Although these purposes are often intertwined as God communicates with us, in this chapter I want to focus specifically on the area of *guidance*—how God gives us direction in our lives.

God also speaks to us in many different ways. However, for the purpose of gaining insight into some of those ways, I will highlight four of them in this chapter: (1) through an inner voice, sometimes called the still small voice; (2) through Scripture;

(3) through other people; and (4) through his peace in our hearts.

It was the prophet Elijah who heard the voice of God as "a gentle whisper" (1 Kings 19:12), or "a still small voice" (KJV). Many Christians have come to use this term for the way in which God guides us through an inner prompting in our hearts. No matter what term we use to describe this subtle voice, it is an experience to which many Christians throughout the ages have given testimony.

One of the times in my own life when God spoke to me in a very clear way through an inner voice was when he first called me to go overseas. In September 1983, while I was in my first semester of college, I was praying in the quietness of my room on what was a very ordinary day. As I was praying, I heard a voice within me say, *Dan, I want you to go to Ashkhabad as a missionary for me one day.*

To my knowledge, I had never even heard the name "Ashkhabad" before that day, so I questioned what I had heard. Maybe I had put too much salsa on my burritos that night. But as I sat in my room, the name "Ashkhabad" kept ringing in my heart. I decided to get up and look at the world map on my wall. Sure enough, there in the south-central part of the Soviet Union was a state called Turkmenia, and its capital city was Ashkhabad. I stood there stunned.

Again I questioned what I had heard. *Could this be for real? Could God be calling me there?* I reasoned further in my own mind, *But the Soviet Union is a closed country. People don't go there as missionaries.*

Despite my initial doubts and questions, I cherished these words as if they were from God. In the days to follow, I eagerly listened for confirmation from God. I wanted to see the writing on the wall. I expected to hear his voice again, to bring clarity to this call. But it never came. I soon realized that I was left with two choices: I could hide the words in my heart and walk in the direction they led, or I could discount the experience altogether and move on. Even though I still had my doubts about the experience, I could not disbelieve that it was actually God who had spoken to me. I chose to hold on to this call from God and to wait patiently for further guidance. I was confident that God had led me to go to college, so I continued my studies, trusting that God would work out the details of this call in his time.

Over the next few years, I went through much testing in regard to this call to serve God in Ashkhabad. As I mentioned the idea to friends, most of them thought that I was crazy and that I should drop it. Many were surprised that I persisted for years to keep the dream alive in my heart. Sometimes being at college in the American Midwest seemed to me to be walking in the opposite direction from this call to Central Asia.

In October of 1991, eight years after the initial experience of hearing God speak to me about Ashkhabad, the world watched as the Soviet Union crumbled and various states became independent countries, Turkmenistan being one of them. In those events I could not help seeing a door opening for me.

Less than a year later, in September 1992, my opportunity came. I will never forget the occasion when I first flew into Ashkhabad. I landed at the airport about 3 a.m. As I got out of the plane, I knelt down on the tarmac and wept. With tears streaming down my face, I looked up to heaven and prayed, "Lord, nine years ago you told me that I would come here. Though I doubted it many times and others laughed, today I am here. Thank you, Jesus, for letting me hear your voice and for fulfilling your words to me." (Although I was only there for two days on that first trip, I've returned there on several occasions to spend prolonged times of service.)

When God speaks to us through an inner voice, it may often be easy to disregard it as merely the product of our imaginations. At any given time, our minds are flooded with a variety of ideas and impressions. But as we practice listening and responding to these special promptings, we learn to distinguish the sound of God's voice in the midst of all the other sounds.

We can never force *God to speak to us, though sometimes we may try.*

For many Christians, one of the most common ways that God speaks is directly through a passage of Scripture. It happens in various ways, but often, when the Scriptures are being read, a certain portion will come alive for you and speak directly to your heart. Somehow God uses that Scripture to uniquely address your own situation. Sometimes, as well, while we are praying or thinking, God will cause us to recall a specific passage of Scripture that will speak to us in a particular way, or God may bring to mind a certain portion of Scripture that we are then to share with someone else, for their encouragement.

Of course we can never *force* God to speak to us, though sometimes we may try. When I was in high school, I attended a prayer meeting where we were encouraged to wait on the Lord in silence. As we did, I was determined to receive a scripture from God. Sure enough, the words *Obadiah, verse 9* popped into my head. *Wow!* I thought to myself, *this actually works. It must be from God because it's such an obscure verse.* As I looked it up, it became obvious to me in my spirit that it wasn't from God at all. Although I laughed at myself, I also realized how inappropriate and ridiculous it was to try to *make* God speak to me.

On another occasion, while I was in prison, God spoke to me through the Scriptures in a very profound and comforting way. On the twenty-first day of my imprisonment, I just had this sense that God wanted me to open my Bible and that he would speak to me. So I grabbed my Bible, and it opened to the tenth chapter of Daniel. Immediately my eyes focused on verses 12 and 13, and I was amazed at what I read: "Do not be afraid, Daniel. Since the first day that you set your mind to gain understanding and to humble yourself before your God, your words were heard, and I have come in response to them. But the prince of the Persian kingdom [which was centered in modern-day Iran] resisted me twenty-one days. Then Michael, one of the chief princes, came to help me, because I was detained there with the king of Persia." God was speaking directly into my situation at that moment and giving me hope. It is amazing how comforting that was for me while I sat alone in prison.

We cannot expect God to speak to us in the same way each time we open the Scriptures. Sometimes, as we read, we may simply grow in our understanding of God's truth. This also is the work of God's Spirit and is certainly no less an impartation of God's grace. Any time that God's truth shines into our hearts, we could say that we are *hearing* God's voice. But there are times when the Holy Spirit addresses a specific scripture to a specific situation in our lives, and we find ourselves being spoken to in a more decisive way.

A third way that God speaks to us is through other people. God uses friends, parents, pastors, and others in our lives to make known his will to us. Their wisdom and advice is God's way of leading and guiding us.

Four years ago I was leading a group on an outreach into Tibet. We arrived in Kathmandu, Nepal, and prepared to go overland from there to Lhasa, the capital of Tibet. Before we left for Tibet, one of my friends on the team, Jerome, came to me and asked if we could smuggle Tibetan Bibles into Lhasa. Without hesitation I told Jerome that it wouldn't be wise because it could cause us problems at the border. But later that night, as I was seeking the Lord, I came under strong conviction that I had made that decision out of fear rather than faith. The truth was that

I didn't really want to pray about it because I didn't want to deal with the danger we could be in through defying the authorities this way. As I confessed my reluctance to God and began to pray for this situation, it became clear to me that I should listen to what God was speaking through Jerome and plan to smuggle the Bibles into Tibet.

As we left Kathmandu, each of us on the team had about five Tibetan Bibles packed into the bottom of our backpacks. At the border we passed by all the guards and officials without any problem, and once we arrived in Lhasa, we were able to distribute the Bibles.

As we seek God for guidance and commit our ways to him, we get a sense of peace.

The Scriptures, of course, are filled with examples of people speaking on God's behalf, sometimes even without their awareness of it. However, as in the above example, we must also discern within ourselves whether or not the words of the other person are meant to be taken as divinely appointed for us.

A fourth way that God speaks to us is simply through the presence of his peace in our hearts. Of course God's peace should be present in our hearts however God is speaking to us, but often, as we seek God for guidance and commit our ways to him, we get a sense of peace about pursuing a certain direction and that is enough for our decision. This is by far the most common way that God makes his will known to us. I'm sure that most of us could think of many examples from our own lives of how God has guided us in this way. Of course it also needs to be said that it is often the absence of God's peace that helps us to know that some options are not to be pursued.

I had a profound experience of this latter scenario a few years ago. Several months before I visited Iran and was subsequently imprisoned, I was visiting my sister Christina in New Delhi, India. After much prayer together, Christina and I decided that we would take a short trip into Iran. We proceeded to acquire our visas and purchase our airline tickets. However, three days before we were to leave, I no longer had any peace in my heart about making the trip. After some questioning and testing, I was still faced with this lack of peace. After another day of waiting, I knew I had to back out. I couldn't make a trip like this without a sense of God's peace. Although my decision made things difficult for my sister and for our relationship, we canceled the trip. One week later Christina found out that she was a couple of weeks pregnant. It is very likely that if we had gone together into Iran at that point, we would have both ended up in prison, as I did months later. I am so thankful to God that he withheld his peace and prevented us from going at that earlier date. As it turned out, it was during my imprisonment some eight and a half months later that Christina had a baby boy, who was given *Daniel* as his middle name to honor the uncle he might never meet.

It should be noted here that a lack of peace is very different from fear. Both can prevent us from pursuing a certain option, and from someone else's perspective, the difference may be hard to detect. In our own hearts, however, the difference should be quite clear. Whereas fear grips our hearts and paralyzes us, a lack of peace sets our hearts free and enables us to look at other options. When we give in to fear, we are left with guilt; when we respond to a lack of peace, we quickly discover a new sense of peace as we explore a different path.

As we seek to hear God's voice, we need to remember that God leads us in different ways at different times in our lives. There is no one "right" way for him to guide us, better than any other. It is entirely up to him to choose just how he will make known his will to us in a particular situation. We simply need to remain sensitive to the many ways there are of hearing from God.

We need to hold on to what God has spoken to us and walk in the direction in which he has led us.

I have also found that often, after God guides us in a specific direction, we experience a time of testing. At that point we need to persevere. We need to hold on to what God has spoken to us and walk in the direction in which he has led us. This also seems to be the occasion when the enemy comes in to tempt us and to misdirect us. Just as the serpent tempted Eve, so the enemy would come to us with the question, "Did God really say…?" We must be aware of the schemes of the enemy and resist him. If we persevere in faith, we will see the promises of God fulfilled.

On rare occasions, as we are walking in obedience to what God has already spoken to us, God will speak again and alter our direction. This experience really puts our trust in God to the test, but hopefully we come through it with a stronger faith in him.

This is seen clearly in the story of Abraham and Isaac, in Genesis 22. God had fulfilled his promise to Abraham and Sarah and miraculously provided them with a son. Isaac was the promised child through whom God's plan of salvation would be carried on. But then God tested Abraham and asked him to sacrifice Isaac as a burnt offering. In an amazing act of trust, Abraham took his young son up a mountain, built an altar, arranged wood upon it, and then bound Isaac to the top. As Abraham took hold of the knife to slay his son, the angel of the Lord stopped him. Abraham clearly having passed the test, God told him not to touch the boy and instead provided a ram for the offering.

In 1989, while I was working in Afghanistan, I also had an experience when God tested me through altering his guidance. I had only been there for four months when the Soviets announced their intention to withdraw their forces from the country. Anticipating the ensuing civil unrest between the various local factions, many of the foreigners working in the country began to evacuate. The organization I was working for decided officially to support the evacuation of foreigners, though they allowed each worker to make his or her own decision. We were asked only to let them know by a certain date what we had decided.

I will never forget the struggle that I went through trying to reach a decision. Why would I leave the Afghans whom I had just come to serve? But why would I stay in this troubled place if most of my team was leaving? It was only after many intense hours of struggle that I decided I would stay.

However, the very next day the American embassy announced that they would be closing their doors, and they strongly encouraged all Americans within the country to leave. This pushed me again to prayer, and I asked the Lord for confirmation regarding my decision. Without any delay and as clear as I have ever heard God, he said, *Dan, I want you to leave.*

Immediately I asked, "But Lord, I thought that you wanted me to stay?"

My son, he answered, *I want you to go. I did ask you to stay, to see to what extent you would be willing to obey me, but now that I know I have your heart, you can go. I don't want you to experience the hardships that you will experience if you stay.* Tears welled up in my eyes as God's love flooded my heart. Oh, how he loved me and cared for me in the deepest of ways.

Whatever means God is using to speak guidance into our lives, it is a unique opportunity for God to deepen our trust in him. This is especially evident when there is a change in guidance—our trust is put to the test, as well as our ability to hear from God.

Although we have identified a wide variety of ways that God speaks to us in the area of guidance, sometimes we still struggle to hear from God. And sometimes God may not be speaking to us in the way we want to hear him. Again, we need to be reminded that God is the one who chooses when and how he will speak. We cannot force him to speak to us in a certain way or at a certain time. Sometimes we may go through times of silence when God is testing us.

When this happens in your life, I would encourage you not to give up hope but to stay focused on God. Honor and glorify him with all your heart. Even in the silence, he is worthy of our worship and our complete surrender. Spend time in the Scriptures and recommit yourself to obey all that is revealed to you. Also, commit yourself to be involved in the last thing you knew for sure that God was leading you to do. Don't be quick to move on to something else until it's clear that God is asking you to move on. Recently I had a sense that God was leading me to move away from Colorado, but as I began to walk toward it, nothing came together. So I simply went back to what I was already doing, in the place that I was doing it.

In times of silence, we need to be reminded that one of the main ways God leads us is through our desires. Psalms 37:4 says, "Delight yourself in the LORD and he will give you the desires of your heart." When our hearts are surrendered to God, then increasingly our desires conform to his will; we begin to desire what God desires for us, and it pleases God to bless us with what we want. Of course sometimes we need to die to our own selfish desires and dedicate ourselves afresh to the purposes and plans of God. But more often than not our decision-making process as Christians is very practical. We ask God to guide us, and we commit our ways to him. Then, with a keen awareness of God's peace upon us, we do what is in our hearts to do.

Moreover, God remains faithful to us whether or not we are conscious of hearing his voice. God is gracious, and he works with us even when we don't understand his leading in our lives. Even when we are completely unaware of it, he is faithfully and gently leading us. It's not all up to us. We need a revelation of God's sovereignty, that he is watching over our affairs and orchestrating our lives according to his good purpose. As the Hebrew proverb affirms,

"In his heart a man plans his course, but the LORD determines his steps" (Prov. 16:9). Ultimately God is in control. Man's responsibility finds its limits within God's sovereignty.

---

*If our hearts are for God,
then it's virtually impossible to
miss his will for our lives.*

I sincerely hope that these insights put our minds at ease somewhat as we seek understanding of God's will for our lives. This is certainly a big question among Christians today, and in some ways we're often too preoccupied with the prospect of missing God's will. If our hearts are for God, then it's virtually impossible to miss his will for our lives. A leader once told me, "The only way to miss the will of God is to know it without a doubt, then go in the other direction." If we are not walking in blatant disobedience, then we probably just need to relax in the arms of God and live our lives for him.

When uncertainty persists as we pray for guidance from God, I have found it helpful to ask three simple questions concerning our options:

1. What would be the most honoring to God?
2. What would Jesus do?
3. What would be the most loving to the other people involved?

These questions won't necessarily lead us to specific answers in every difficult situation, but it is amazing to me how often they have helped me make decisions when I wasn't sure what to do.

Remember, most of all God desires friendship with us, and guidance is something that flows from a place of intimacy with him. Sometimes, when we are desperate for guidance we can actually become self-absorbed in our effort to hear from God. We can become so fixated with making the right decision that we actually push God aside. At times like that, we need to be careful that our desire for guidance doesn't distract us from the simple pleasures of our relationship with God.

In closing, I just want to emphasize that all who follow God will hear his voice in some way or another. Hearing from God is not just for the missionary or the pastor. God wants to speak to his people whatever their vocation, whether they are in business, in school, or at home. God is committed to having his voice heard by us. I sincerely hope that as you finish this chapter, you will be refreshed and excited about the prospect of hearing from God. Again, as the metaphor of sheep with a shepherd affirms, hearing God's voice comes from spending time with him. As we invest in our relationship with God, our trust in him will be deepened and we will be inspired to give ourselves wholeheartedly to him. From that place of intimate trust, then, we will also be ready to give ourselves genuinely to others.

🍃 part three

Serving

The final two chapters of this book focus on serving. Service is the natural overflow of a life surrendered to God. As we give ourselves to God, he delights in using us to positively affect the lives of others around us. When we align our hearts with this godly purpose, through believing and trusting in him, we find ourselves serving. In chapter 7 we will look at the most important and basic way we serve, loving people, and in chapter 8 we will look at our availability and readiness to serve.

And now these three remain: faith, hope and love. But the greatest of these is love.

—1 Corinthians 13:13

Dear friends, let us love one another, for love comes from God.

—1 John 4:7

chapter six

Loving People

*J*esus not only calls us into relationship with himself but into relationship with others. Loving God inevitably leads us to loving people. The apostle Paul was a man who loved God, and it was that love that compelled him to spend his life in service to others. In his letter to the Philippians, Paul takes an honest look at his own life, and he explains that, in one way, he would rather die so that he could be united with Christ; but if God chose to allow him to remain alive, then Paul would live not for himself but for the sake of others (1:22–26). Paul loved people.

This is exactly what Jesus modeled as well. In Mark 10:45, Jesus explains that he "did not come to be served, but to serve, and to give his life as a ransom for many." Jesus knew exactly what his mission in life was. He lived, and died, for the benefit of others. We ourselves have no better example to follow. The more secure we are in ourselves and in our relationship with God, the freer we are to serve others. True spiritual maturity is tested in our relationships with others.

---

*This is what life is all about:
loving God and loving people.*

This is very much in line with how Jesus defined the chief responsibilities in life. One day, when he was being questioned by the Pharisees, a lawyer from among them asked him, "'Teacher, which is the greatest commandment in the Law?'

"Jesus replied: '"Love the Lord your God with all your heart and with all your soul and with all your mind." This is the first and greatest commandment. And the second is like it: "Love your neighbor as yourself." All the Law and the Prophets hang on these two commandments'" (Matt. 22:34–40).

These two commandments summarize what God has required of us. They get to the heart of what life is all about: loving God and loving people. What a beautiful thing Jesus has done to clarify our lives. Can it really be that simple? Yes, it can.

When you wake up in the morning and don't know what to do, just ask yourself how you can love God and love people. It isn't always easy to know exactly *how* to love, but these two simple responsibilities certainly give us the right focus. They require us to continually return to God and ask, "How can I show love in this situation, toward you and toward others?" This is the life that Jesus lived. This is the life that he calls us to live.

While I was in college, God challenged me through this scripture to get outside of myself and into the lives of others. I tended to be quiet and reserved, and sometimes I would use that as an excuse to be self-centered. But I decided to make a commitment to ask a simple question in prayer every morning, "God, how can I love people today?" It was difficult, especially at first, but week by week it became easier, and slowly I learned how to love the people that God brought into my life. After six months I took some time to evaluate. First, I had found that the more I focused on loving others, the more joy I had in my life. Second, I realized how much I had grown in certain areas of my character without even focusing on them. I found that I had more patience for people and that my mind was no longer filled with worries about my future, my finances, and my reputation. It was just as Jesus explained in the Beatitudes: "You're blessed when you care. At the moment of being 'care-full,' you find yourselves cared for" (Matt. 5:7, MSG). It was so refreshing for me to focus on the simple responsibility of loving others and to allow God to work on other areas of personal growth in my life.

*We need to learn to embrace
the present moment.*

One of the realities of this lifestyle is that our time and energies become more and more focused on "the now." We learn to embrace the present moment. We learn to pay attention to what God is doing in each and every situation, especially in the lives of those around us. This goes against the grain. So often we live our lives either in the future or in the past. We are consumed with what we should have done or what we should do. We are plagued with guilt and worry, and we end up being distracted, unable to engage what is before us in the present. How often do we miss an opportunity to really pay attention to someone or to listen to what God may be speaking to us through someone else? We are so preoccupied with our own concerns that we miss out on real life.

Jesus met people where they were.

As usual, the example of Jesus is inspiring and instructive for us. Look at the way in which he was able to be *with* people. He gave them his undivided attention. Consider the Samaritan woman at the well (John 4), or the belligerent blind man (Mark 10:46–52) or the thief on the cross (Luke 23:39–43) or the many, many others who wanted his attention. Jesus graciously gave it, and in most cases he granted their requests. He met people where they were. Jesus loved people.

Think about how two lovers interact. They cherish every moment with each other. They are consumed with each other. Nothing else matters. The moment is everything. They pay attention to each other with everything that is within them. Though we cannot expect the same level of emotion to infuse every encounter with others, we can learn to love in a way that communicates sincere respect and appreciation. We need to ask ourselves if we have a genuine interest in people. Do people matter to us? How do people feel when they're with us? Do they feel loved and accepted?

We need to put others first and trust that Jesus will provide for our own needs.

When someone really pays attention to me in a one-on-one encounter, it makes me feel very good and means a lot to me. One man that has modeled this to me very effectively has been Floyd McClung. He is serving as a pastor now, but formerly he was one of my leaders in YWAM. Although he was a very busy man with much responsibility, whenever I met with him, he gave me his undivided attention. He made me feel important and loved, as if our conversation was all that mattered to him at that moment.

One of the greatest ways to show love to others is to listen to them. We all need people in our lives who listen to us, people with whom we can share our hearts. But we also need to be this kind of person for others. We need the grace to love in this way. We need to put others first and trust that Jesus will provide for our own needs. Jesus says, "Give, and it will be given to you" (Luke 6:38), and this is true in relationships. We may often feel like we don't have much to give. We may feel that we need the attention ourselves. But as we reach out to others and serve them, we will discover that God is also caring for us and meeting our needs.

God wants to expand our capacity to love.

Sometimes when we meet lots of people, we are tempted to shut some of them out. We think we cannot handle any more. The demands seem to be too much. We feel that there are natural limits on our ability to love. I, too, have found at times that I just couldn't love any more than I already was. In those times I thought that I had only so much love to give. I imagined that my capacity to love was like a pie— if I was loving four people and God brought me four more, then my love was divided into eight portions, each one now receiving only half the love that the original four had received. This caused me much frustration, and I struggled to understand God's perspective on it. Then one day God shed some light on the issue for me. He helped me see that God, rather than simply accepting my limitations in loving, wanted to *expand* my capacity to love. Then I would be able to love all eight people to the same extent as I had loved the original four. Of course it didn't mean that I was able to spend as much time with each one, but it did mean that in my heart I was able to find room for more people and love them in the way that God wanted.

It is important for us to value each and every person God brings into our lives and to make an investment in each one, whoever he or she is, whatever the situation. As I have had the opportunity to travel, God has allowed me to meet many people, some for as short as a minute, others for a much longer time. Even though sometimes it's been hard for me to say goodbye to old friends, and equally hard sometimes to give myself wholeheartedly to new people in my life, God has challenged me to reach out in love to others, whether or not I will ever see them again. The fact is, as people step out of our lives, we never know if we will get another opportunity to see them. But if we have made an investment in a relationship, then we are able to pick up right where we left off when we get the chance to meet them again. I have found this to be a great blessing in my life. I left my full-time post in Kabul, Afghanistan, in 1993, but ever since then I have taken every opportunity to return there. God has allowed me numerous opportunities, and I have been able to deepen existing relationships and build new ones there. Kabul and its people will always be a part of my life.

What should we do when we get hurt? Jesus invites us to run to him.

Sometimes people's ability to love others is restricted because of past hurts. Often, when we get hurt in relationships, we try to protect ourselves the next time we face a similar situation. We aren't quite as willing to make ourselves vulnerable. We guard our hearts. I have struggled with this and have often allowed my hurt to diminish my capacity to love others. What should we do when we get hurt? Jesus invites us to run to him. The more I run to him in these situations, the more he is able to meet my deepest needs and restore my capacity to love. Jesus commands us to love our neighbor, no matter how difficult that may be. It is a command without conditions. When we find it hard to reach out to others with love, let us remember both the commands of Jesus and his example. He will give us the grace to obey.

When I have been hurt and tempted to withhold my love from others, I have often recalled the wise words of my youth pastor. He said, "It is better to love and get hurt than not love at all." This is just another area in our lives in which we are called to die to ourselves and to choose Jesus above our own insecurities. Even though it has been tough, I have experienced God's blessing time and again as I have made myself vulnerable and made the choice to love. It has brought great joy to my heart, and it has kept me open and tender not only before God but before others as well. As I have become more involved in the lives of others, I have learned so much about the character of Jesus through these relationships. Oh, that we would understand the tragedy of closing ourselves off from others due to past hurts. It leads only to isolation and further pain.

Our commitment to relationships is frequently tested. One of the greatest challenges in loving others is in seeking to restore relationships that have been damaged or even broken off. God's heart is always to repair and restore, and we need to believe that God is able to do this with the difficult relationships in our lives. I have had such relationships in my own life, even with family members, but I have experienced God's commitment to reconciliation and restoration in all relationships that have somewhere gone wrong.

Even in the midst of personal crisis,
Jesus modeled servanthood for us,
and he calls us to follow.

Jesus has shown us his commitment to relationships through servanthood. He modeled it for us over and over again, but perhaps nowhere else was it displayed so beautifully as at the Last Supper, when he washed the feet of his disciples. During the evening meal Jesus got up and dressed himself as a typical servant, taking off his outer clothing and wrapping a towel around his waist. Then he poured water into a basin, and kneeling before each disciple one by one, he washed their feet. This was Jesus' final opportunity to be with his friends in such an intimate setting. He was in great need himself. His heart was heavy with what lay ahead, and yet he reached out to serve. He displayed his great love for his disciples through active and humble service. Even in the midst of personal crisis, Jesus modeled servanthood for us, and he calls us to follow: "Now that I, your Lord and Teacher, have washed your feet, you also should wash one another's feet. I have set you an example that you should do as I have done for you" (John 13:14–15).

We see this also stated clearly in Paul's letter to the Philippians, where Paul exhorts, "Your attitude should be the same as that of Christ Jesus: Who, being in very nature God, did not consider equality with God something to be grasped, but made himself nothing, taking the very nature of a servant, being made in human likeness" (2:5–7). Jesus laid it all down for us. He lowered himself for us.

Jesus calls us to embrace not only the easy to love, the obvious objects of our affection, but the difficult people in our lives as well.

How do we love our neighbor? We become servants. We give up our own rights and desires for the sake of others. We humble ourselves and give our lives in service. If that's what Jesus did for us, should we do any less for others? If we follow his example, we will find ways to serve—to honor others and put their desires above our own.

Jesus teaches us that loving our neighbor also includes loving our enemies. Jesus makes this very clear in the Sermon on the Mount:

> But I tell you who hear me: Love your enemies, do good to those who hate you, bless those who curse you, pray for those who mistreat you.... If you love those who love you, what credit is that to you? Even "sinners" love those who love them. And if you do good to those who are good to you, what credit is that to you? Even "sinners" do that.... But love your enemies, do good to them, and lend to them without expecting to get anything back. Then your reward will be great, and you will be sons of the Most High, because he is kind to the ungrateful and wicked. Be merciful, just as your Father is merciful (Luke 6:27–36; see also Matt. 5:43–47).

Loving our enemies is not easy. Jesus explains in these verses that it requires something beyond what is natural. It's easier to love those who love us, but to love those who hate us is quite unnatural and definitely difficult. Because of this, it seems that many Christians today fail to obey this command. We want this simple command to mean something other than what it plainly says. We want to justify our hatred and prejudice. But the real problem with this command is not so much in the understanding but in the obeying.

It may be helpful, when considering this challenge to love, to remember that we ourselves may be the "difficult person" in someone else's life!

Jesus calls us to embrace not only the easy to love, the obvious objects of our affection, but the difficult people in our lives as well—even our enemies. This takes loving our neighbor to the farthest limits, in what is truly a test of Christian love. We all have such people in our lives—people we avoid or against whom we hold a grudge. It may be someone at work or perhaps someone at church. Or it may be an extended-family member, perhaps the individual who is, for you, the downside of attending the annual family reunion. Of course it may be helpful, when considering this challenge to love, to remember that

we ourselves may be the "difficult person" in someone else's life! Whatever our personal situation, we
are all challenged to deal with such relationships in
the way that Jesus calls us to: with simple, supernatural love.

The apostle Paul echoes the words of Jesus when
he instructs his readers to "Bless those who persecute
you; bless and do not curse" (Rom. 12:14). He goes
on to underscore his point by quoting Proverbs
25:21: "If your enemy is hungry, feed him; if he is
thirsty, give him something to drink" (vs. 20).

I saw this kind of love in action one day during
Afghanistan's civil war, when I was working in a hospital in Kabul. Intense fighting had broken out on
the city streets. As was our custom on such days, some
of us at the hospital who were foreigners gave the
national workers rides home, as most public transport
had stopped. On this occasion, Bill, a coworker of
mine from New York, and I were dropping off an
Afghan coworker when we found ourselves amidst a
violent skirmish. As we began to retreat, we saw our
Afghan friend being accosted by a local soldier.
Immediately Bill and I recognized that the soldier
was a member of the ethnic group within the country
that had been responsible for recent kidnappings and
killings, an effort to cleanse the nation of a rival

group. Our friend was from that rival group, and this soldier appeared intent on dealing cruelly with him. We also saw the fear in our friend's eyes. Realizing that this situation would most likely end in the execution of our friend and coworker, Bill and I chose to intervene. We got out of our car and attempted to retrieve our friend, but the soldier held on to him firmly. He then turned his RPG (rocket-propelled grenade) directly at us and commanded us to leave at once. With the RPG pointed right at our heads, Bill looked the soldier in the eye and noticed that it was bloodshot. Realizing that he had some eye drops from the hospital in his pocket, Bill asked the soldier, "Does your eye itch?"

With a look of bewilderment, the soldier answered, "Yes." Bill pulled the medication out of his pocket and offered it to the soldier. Setting his gun aside, the soldier reached out his hand to receive the eye drops. Other soldiers, looking on with envy, gathered around to receive medication also. Right there on the street, Bill and I were hosting an eye clinic. Only moments before we had been face to face with an angry and armed soldier. We distributed eye medication to five soldiers, and all of them immediately began to feel better. Not only that, of course, but their moods had been completely transformed. They apologized profusely to us, released our friend, and then invited us for tea. We declined the invitation and, with a great sigh of relief, went on our way, amazed at the power of a love that reaches out to serve.

Jesus not only commanded us to love our enemies, he gave us an example to follow. He himself loved those who hated him.

Jesus not only commanded us to love our enemies, he gave us an example to follow. He himself loved those who hated him. He endured all manner of evil and corruption at the hands of his enemies. Even as Jesus was dying on the cross, he was loving his enemies, asking God to forgive those responsible for his death (Luke 23:34).

In my case, it was during my unjust imprisonment in Iran that I learned more than I could have ever imagined about loving my enemies. From the very first day that I began to be interrogated, God challenged me to love my interrogators. The more hostile they became, the harder the challenge became. On the second day of interrogation, they began to use physical force to persuade me to speak. As they slapped me in the face, I heard the Lord speak to me: *Dan, ask me what I think of this man.*

Initially I thought to myself, *I don't want to know.* But after a few minutes I prayed to heaven and asked, *Lord, what do you think of this man?* As soon as I asked that question, I began to have an overwhelming compassion for my interrogator. My heart broke for him. God gave me a glimpse of his love for this man. This change in my own heart was not of my own doing but truly a miracle. I began to pray for him and to bless him in whatever way I could. The compassion grew in my heart.

The actions of my interrogator didn't change, but I continued to love him, hoping that God was working in his heart. One day, during the sixth week of my imprisonment, the guards came and led me out of my cell. I was terrified, thinking that I was being led to another session of interrogation. This time, however, instead of going downstairs, they led me into a small office. I walked into the office and was given permission to take my blindfold off, and there sat my interrogator behind a desk. As usual the very sight of him struck fear in my heart. He was my enemy. He was the one who had hit me repeatedly and yelled at me over and over again. But this time, as I sat across from him, something began to happen within me. I was supplied with a supernatural boldness. I looked at him and said, "Sir, if I'm going to see you for the rest of my life, why don't we become friends?"

"What?" he said, shaking his head.

I continued, "Sir, I know it's in your heart to become my friend. It's just your job that stops you. You can start by telling me your name." As I said that, I stretched out my hand to shake his. Expecting to get hit or be ridiculed, I was truly amazed at what happened next. It was far more beautiful than I could have imagined. My interrogator did not move, but tears started to well up in his eyes. I watched as the hardness in his face melted away before me. I waited, my hand still outstretched across his desk. His tears continued to flow. Finally he stretched out his hand, grasping mine, and said, "My name is Razaq, Mr. Baumann."

Up to that point I had never heard this man call me by my name; I had simply been "Number 58," the number of my cell.

Razaq continued. "I can't help you get out of here. It's not in my jurisdiction, but maybe I can help you within the prison. I have some influence over the guards. Is there anything you need? Perhaps a better cell?"

I thought for a second, hardly believing what I had just been offered: "Sure, I would like that."

"Then I will see what I can do," he replied.

We continued to talk for fifteen minutes, no longer as enemies but as friends. I was amazed at what was happening right before my eyes. God's love had won Razaq's heart, and he was changed. My interrogator had become my friend. Later that night the guards came and moved me to a better cell.

We believe in a God
who makes friends out of enemies.
Never give up loving.

We believe in a God who makes friends out of enemies. Love will always win in the end. Never give up loving. God can change the hardest of hearts. I had the privilege of seeing God at work that day in prison.

Around the same time, during my imprisonment, I also saw the love of God at work in the lives of my guards. One day I overheard the guards talking at the end of the corridor. They were speaking in Farsi, a language that I had learned in Afghanistan, so I listened carefully as they began to talk about Glenn and me, the foreign prisoners. They began to ask questions among themselves, "Why? Why did they come here, knowing that we kill Christians? And why are they praying prayers of blessing upon those who could kill them?" (I didn't know it, but they had hidden a microphone in my room and had been listening to everything I had been saying, and praying.)

Then one of the guards spoke up and said, "Well, I know what Christians believe." He began to tell the others that he had heard the whole gospel story many years before. He began to tell them about Jesus and why he came. I sat in my room amazed as the guard shared about the love of God.

After three or four days of discussing these things, three of them agreed and said, "These foreigners have a reason for living. They have purpose—a reason to live and a reason to die. They talk about a God of love, and that seems so right. I want to have this same reason and purpose for living."

I sat in my cell as these three guards gave their lives to Jesus in the corridor. Again God had challenged me to love my enemies, and now I was privileged to see how his love had won their hearts.

I saw the same amazing love at work in another man as well, none other than the judge who had all but condemned me to death. I will never forget the day of my release from prison, when that judge read aloud a letter that stated I could be set free. As I turned to walk away from the judge, God showed me yet another incident where his love was victorious. This time the judge approached me, reached out his arms, and drew me close. Then he gave me three kisses, cheek to cheek to cheek, which I knew was a customary greeting between Iranian men but only practiced between good friends. I was stunned. The man who had hated me most, who had been my foremost accuser, and who I had thought of as my greatest enemy in Iran, now had had a change of heart and wanted to become my friend. Again the love of God prevailed.

*When we truly love God,
the lives of those around us will
also experience that love.*

As we continue to discover the depths of God's love for us, we will be set free to be channels of that love to others. When we truly love God, the lives of those around us will also experience that love. This

should be the trademark of the followers of Jesus—
our love for others. As God calls you to love, he will
give you the grace to love, whatever the circumstance.

Then I heard the voice of the Lord saying, "Whom shall I send? And who will go for us?" And I said, "Here am I. Send me!"

—the prophet Isaiah, Isaiah 6:8

My grace is sufficient for you, for my power is made perfect in weakness.

—God's word to Paul, 2 Corinthians 12:9

chapter seven

Ready to Serve

*T*here is no higher calling in this life than to serve the High King of Heaven, the Lord Jesus Christ. As we break free from the various obligations and requirements that we put on ourselves, or that we receive from others, we are set free to respond to our Lord in wholehearted service. We are able to offer ourselves out of inspiration rather than obligation. We are able to say, "Here I am, Lord; I'm ready to serve."

It is not so much my concern in this final chapter to describe the different ways we serve. The previous chapter has identified the most important and basic way—love. Here I want to do all that I can to encourage you to make yourself available to God—to help you remove the obstacles that get in your way and to persuade you to lay down your life for the service of your King.

God has blessed each and every one of us with various abilities. We all have something to offer, something to benefit and further the kingdom of God. As we submit ourselves to Jesus and seek to do his will, we will discover that he is using us. And when you discover that, your life takes on new meaning. What an amazing thing that is: the God of all creation finds people like you and me *useful* for his purpose and for the glory of his name!

Our service to God is the natural
outworking of his life within us.

Service is, in some ways, the ultimate act of surrender. It's not so much what we *do*, but rather what we *allow*. We are allowing God to live through us. It brings to mind again the powerful image from John 15 of a branch bearing fruit—it does so only because of its connection to the vine. It is the vine that gives life to the branch and actually causes the fruit to grow. In the same way, our service to God is the natural outworking of his life within us.

As we think about serving God, then, what could possibly hinder us? One of the statements that I hear again and again as I travel and talk to many Christians is, "Well, I don't feel ready." The importance of *being* ready, or *feeling* ready, is an idea with a strong hold on our culture. This keeps so many Christians from stepping out and making themselves available to God. Yet we have no right to give this excuse of not being ready. We have no right to disqualify ourselves in this way. Jesus said, "Come, follow me, *and I will make you* fishers of men" (Mark 1:17, emphasis added). Jesus will do what is necessary to qualify us and equip us for service. Unless we are walking in blatant disobedience, according to Jesus we are ready to serve.

It is a terrible lie that we must achieve greater levels of holiness and readiness *before* we are able to offer ourselves in service. Jesus is willing to accept us now. We must not put requirements upon ourselves that are not from God. He knows how weak and frail we are, but still he calls us to serve him. He invites us to abandon ourselves to him and to go for it! The apostle Paul agrees: "Not that we are competent in ourselves to claim anything for ourselves, but our competence comes from God. He has made us competent as ministers of a new covenant" (2 Cor. 3:5–6). If we are willing, we will see God do amazing things around us, through us, and in us. We need to allow God to use us even when we don't feel ready. Jesus didn't necessarily feel ready in the Garden of Gethsemane, but he obeyed anyway, saying to the Father, "Not what I will, but what you will" (Mark 14:36). Jesus was willing to trust, and willing to act upon that trust, whatever the consequences.

We are servants of Jesus, and obedience to his call is always our immediate priority.

It is important to remember that God is both our loving Father and our sovereign Lord and Master. We are his children, but we are also his servants, awaiting his instruction, willing to do whatever he asks. We must submit to his wisdom and authority, trusting him to decide when and where he will use us. He will commission us—it is our responsibility to obey.

Sadly enough, because of our insecurities and lack of trust, we are not always ready to obey. Sometimes we even allow our understanding of personal giftedness to distract us from what Jesus is calling us to do at that moment. As we discover our gifts, sometimes we become preoccupied with a particular gift, and then we neglect opportunities to serve that don't seem to immediately fit that gift category. We say, "I'm a teacher, so I won't take this opportunity in evangelism." Or we think, "I have leadership gifts, so that task is below me." All the while we are resisting the prompting of Jesus and missing out on an opportunity to serve. We need to remember that we are servants of Jesus and obedience to his call is always our immediate priority.

God is longing to give away his life and love to a hurting world, and he wants to do that through us.

Sometimes people use other excuses for not being ready. One is education: "I need a college degree before I'll serve God." Another is the great delay: "Give me a couple years, and then I'll be ready." Desperately we give excuses, often to cover up our fears and anxieties. Whatever our reasons, we are unwilling to obey the call of God. We forget that he has chosen us to accomplish his will in the world.

Whatever our issues, whatever we are struggling with, God has chosen to work with us. God is longing to give away his life and love to a hurting world, and he wants to do that through us. He wants to use you.

Now, of course, God may lead us to attend college or to spend a year or more doing this or that. But we should do so only in obedience to his leading, not as an excuse to avoid or delay obedience. I spent four years in college to earn a degree in business administration, and afterward I went off to Afghanistan to work in hospital administration. Was serving in Afghanistan the goal and going to college the preparation? No, I didn't see it that way. Both tasks were, for me, steps of obedience. I was simply doing the next thing that I felt Jesus had asked me to do. If he had asked me to go to college, then that's where I would live for him and serve him until he called me elsewhere. I had a rich spiritual life at college. I had many opportunities to serve people, to build friendships, and to grow in my relationship with Jesus. I wouldn't trade that time for anything. If I had been preoccupied during those years with going overseas, I might have missed out on all that. When I finally did get the opportunity to go to Afghanistan, I received it from God simply as another opportunity to love him and serve others. It was the next thing I felt called to do. All along our journey, wherever we are, whatever we are doing, we need to have a sense of calling, that we are being obedient to God's will, eager and ready to serve.

We need to offer ourselves in wholehearted service despite our fears and insecurities.

The apostle Paul didn't always feel ready. We sometimes imagine him as a man of great skill and confidence. But in his first letter to the Corinthians he admits to something quite different: "When I came to you, brothers, I did not come with eloquence or superior wisdom as I proclaimed to you the testimony about God.... I came to you in weakness and fear, and with much trembling" (1 Cor. 2:1–3). Paul was nervous. He felt insecure. He wasn't confident in his speaking abilities. He had issues just like you and I. But he doesn't appear to be hindered by some notion of readiness. Despite his insecurities, he served wholeheartedly. And in Paul's mind, his weaknesses helped to clarify the divine origin of his message: "My message and my preaching were not with wise and persuasive words, but with a demonstration of the Spirit's power, so that your faith might not rest on men's wisdom, but on God's power" (vss. 4–5).

What if Paul had waited until he felt ready before he brought the gospel to Corinth? Would he ever have gone? In the same way, the world waits for us to come to them even in our weakness. Like Paul, we need to offer ourselves in wholehearted service despite our fears and insecurities. God's grace will be sufficient for us.

However, many of us allow our feelings to rule our lives, even when it comes to decisions about serving God. Sometimes we give in to apathy. We don't fully give ourselves to God's service, simply because we don't want to, we don't feel like it. As petty as it sounds, it hinders our service, not to mention our relationship with God.

I have struggled with these feelings in my own life. When I first arrived in Afghanistan I didn't feel like being there. I was confident that God had led me there, but I was lacking a sense of purpose and passion. Instead I felt hesitant and inadequate. My early days there were difficult, but as I began to settle in to my situation, a sense of urgency came over me to pray for the people of Kabul and the work there. I began to walk through the city streets and to pray as I walked. I did this every day for at least an hour, and within weeks I was beginning to experience a miracle within me. Slowly but surely God was giving me a heart for the people of Kabul and a passion for the work of his kingdom there. After three months my heart was completely there and there was no other place that I would have rather been. I spent the next several years there, excited about the opportunity that God had given me to serve him.

That love for Afghanistan continues to grow even today. I am so thankful to God that he not only allowed me to live in Afghanistan for those years but also gave me a piece of his heart for the Afghan people. And to think that I could have missed out on all that if I had chosen to follow my feelings from the beginning rather than the call of God.

As Christians we are constantly faced with decisions like this. Our feelings often scream out to us and plead with us to choose what feels better, which can often be against the way of God. But we don't have to give in to our feelings. It's never easy to choose against them, but the more we do it, the easier it becomes. It is a constant challenge, but as we walk with God day by day, we can learn to choose his ways over our feelings. I have also found that the more I choose God's ways, the more I begin to see

God's goodness and love in those ways. I begin to see how unreliable my feelings actually are and how they are able to distract me from choosing what is God's best for my life. When we do give in to our feelings, which I have often done, we end up forfeiting the freedom and joy that God wants to bless us with. We only need to trust in him.

It is important that we are able to see the difference between these personal feelings that distract us and the desires of our hearts that guide us. Both come from within us, yet they have a very different effect on us. Those feelings that distract us from obedience will grate on us. They pull us down, and when we give in to them, we know we are settling for something less. They align themselves easily with fears and insecurities, and they are dealt with only as we face them honestly and choose to rise above them. In contrast, as discussed in chapter 5, the godly desires of our hearts speak within us as viable options for our path. They present themselves clearly, and instead of bringing confusion, they help us to discern a certain direction. Ultimately, instead of distracting us from obedience, these desires in our hearts express precisely what it is that God is calling us to do at the moment. In them, we have aligned our hearts with God's heart.

I learned a lot from Glenn, my friend and fellow prisoner in Iran, about living by faith and not by feelings. Although we were imprisoned together, we were immediately separated, and it was only on the day of his release, some five weeks later, that we were able to spend a couple of hours together. During that time Glenn shared with me about how God had led him to meditate on Philippians 4:8 during his imprisonment: "Finally, brothers, whatever is true, whatever is noble, whatever is right, whatever is pure, whatever is lovely, whatever is admirable—if anything is excellent or praiseworthy—think about such things." Any time that thoughts and feelings caused Glenn to dwell on something other than what fit into this verse, he chose to put it out of his mind and to focus only on good things. At first this was very difficult, but as he practiced it, slowly he was able to discipline his mind in this direction. He found that as he persevered in this, his mind was being renewed. He experienced the truth of Paul's challenge in Romans 12:2, "Do not conform any longer to the pattern of this world, but be transformed by the renewing of your mind." As Glenn experienced this transformation in his mind, his feelings followed and came under his control. For him it was one of the most important things he learned in prison.

What about when we fail miserably and feel unworthy to be called a servant of Jesus? What about when we fall into sin in the midst of serving? At that moment our greatest need is to repent. We confess our sins to God and receive his forgiveness. For many of us, it is difficult to move on. We tend to grovel in our guilt. For example, if I sin in the area of lust, I usually feel guilty about it and not worthy of serving God for at least a day or two. I feel dirty. And often, by the time I start feeling on top of things, I stumble again—and the cycle continues. In these situations, it's almost as if we feel we need to pay the price for our own mistakes. Somehow we think we can earn God's forgiveness. But we are very wrong—we cannot earn this gift.

{God} does not treat us as our sins deserve or repay us according to our iniquities. —Psalm 103:10

David was a great man of God who fell into sexual sin while he was serving God as king of Israel. In Psalm 103 David delights in the grace of God when he affirms that "[God] does not treat us as our sins deserve or repay us according to our iniquities" (vs. 10). So often, when things don't go well for us, we imagine that God is somehow getting back at us for what we have done wrong. God is not like that. He does not treat us as our sins deserve. When we become aware of our sinful state, we naturally feel that we deserve to be treated like lousy sinners. But God loves to forgive us. He loves to accept us, even though we don't deserve it. God wants desperately to take away the very thing that keeps us in our guilt and separates us from him. It is as David explains two verses later in the same psalm: "As far as the east is from the west, so far has he removed our transgressions from us" (Ps. 103:12). God has removed our sin from the picture. He wants us to enjoy unhindered fellowship with him. He wants us to enjoy the freedom that he has accomplished for us on the cross: "So if the Son sets you free, you will be free indeed" (John 8:36).

*Keep company with me and you'll
learn to live freely and lightly.
—Jesus in Matthew 11:30 (MSG)*

This is the kind of freedom that is available to all who follow Jesus. In Matthew 11:28–30, Jesus says, "Are you tired? Worn out? Burned out on religion? Come to me. Get away with me and you'll recover your life. I'll show you how to take a real rest. Walk with me and work with me—watch how I do it. Learn the unforced rhythms of grace. I won't lay anything heavy or ill-fitting on you. Keep company with me and you'll learn to live freely and lightly" (MSG). When Jesus says, "work with me," he is inviting us to serve. When we choose to follow Jesus and to serve him, we are embarking on *a beautiful way*. It is a life that is full of refreshing fellowship and learning.

The more I understand God's love for me, the more I want to offer my life in service.

God never meant for our obedience and service to be a chore. It is meant to be the natural overflow of enjoying our relationship with him. As I was once told, "Everything we do for God will be the overflow of intimacy with God." More than anything else, love is what motivates service. The more I understand

God's love for me, the more I want to love him back, the more I want to offer my life in service. The deeper the love, the deeper the commitment and the less our feelings will work against us. In other words, as we become more and more focused on Jesus, our desire to please him takes precedence over our other desires. As a result, feelings that once distracted us from our obedience to Jesus now have less and less of an effect on our hearts. There is victory for each one of us over our feelings but only in the context of relationship, only as we accept the invitation that Jesus extends to us.

Are you ready to serve? If Christ lives within you, then nothing can stop you.

Are you ready to serve? If Christ lives within you, then nothing can stop you. It doesn't matter whether you are young or old, whether you are working in a career or going to school or staying at home, God wants to use you for his glory, and he will give you opportunities to serve. If you understand his personal love for you and believe in your heart that he is good, then what could possibly stand in your way?

Center your life on him, and your choices will reflect his priorities. Learn to trust in him as you encounter fears. Spend time listening to his voice and walk in obedience to it. As your life becomes consumed with Jesus, let his life and love flow through you to the people around you. If you do this, the world will never be the same again. You will see God's kingdom come here on earth as it is in heaven.

What is our reward? Is it happiness? Fulfillment? Success? No, even though we may experience these, none of these is guaranteed to those who serve Jesus. The reward *is* Jesus—Jesus himself and our relationship with him. If that doesn't seem like it's enough, then you don't know him. You don't yet understand the true value of knowing Jesus. You have not yet found a beautiful way. You have not yet found the treasure in the field that you would joyfully give up everything else to acquire (Matt. 13:44). Everything else comes and goes, but Jesus is always with us. The more you know Jesus, the more you know that nothing else compares. The encouragement for each one of us is that the invitation to experience more of Jesus is still being given. We need only to accept it.

What happens within us as we stand before a beautiful sunset? Do we strive to enjoy it? No, we just relax and enjoy the beauty. When we stand before Jesus, do we strive to enjoy him? No, again we need only to embrace the beauty and enjoy it. We're already there before Jesus. In striving we are only giving in to distractions. We become restless. We are trying to change something to make the moment better, to put something else in order before we can enjoy it. Instead we need to stop and simply enjoy. It is finished. All is ready. The door is open. Come and enjoy. Jesus is more beautiful than anything else you have ever seen or heard or experienced. He waits for you to embrace him. He invites you now to enjoy him forever.

✸ about the authors

To contact Dan Baumann and Mark Klassen, please email them at abeautifulway@hotmail.com.

Dan Baumann is presently serving with Youth With A Mission in Trinidad, Colorado. As a community, he and his coworkers are committed to discipling young people and seeing God worshiped in the nations of the earth. The Rocky Mountain Discipleship School is a five-month program with three months of training and a two-month outreach. If you would like more information, please visit www.ywamcolorado.org. If you would like to learn more about Dan's harrowing experiences in Iran, his book *Imprisoned in Iran* tells the story.

Mark Klassen is a personal friend of Dan Baumann. He served for several years with Youth With A Mission and was involved with YWAM's School of Biblical Studies in various locations around the Pacific and Asia. Mark has a bachelor's degree in Biblical Studies from YWAM's University of the Nations and a master's degree in Old Testament from Regent College in Vancouver, B.C., Canada. He presently lives in Yarrow, B.C., with his wife, Amy, and their two daughters, Alexis and Dania.